Praise for *Dreaming through Darkness*:

'Charlie Morley has produced not just a self-help book but a guide
to befriending all of who you truly are. Charlie is the real deal,
and this book is like being led down a full spiritual journey by an
old and jovial friend. An honest, compassionate and enjoyable
read that will lead to incredible self-acceptance and joy.'
Lodro Rinzler, author of The Buddha Walks into a Bar and Love Hurts

'With great lucidity, Charlie Morley show us how, instead
of hiding from our shadow, rejecting it or indulging it, we
can in fact integrate it so that we achieve much greater
wholeness and personal freedom. I learned so much from
this book and know I will return to it time and time again.'
**David R. Hamilton PhD, author of How Your Mind Can
Heal Your Body and The Five Side Effects of Kindness**

'I have known Charlie for a long time and I consider
him a very positive influence in the world. In this book
he guides people in how to be more helpful human
beings. I strongly believe his authentic confidence
and sound mind give him the ability to do this.'
Lama Yeshe Rinpoche, Abbot of Samye Ling Monastery

'To dare to go into the dark I need a guide I know I can trust.
Charlie Morley is that guide. What I love most about this
wonderful book is Charlie's courage in authentically sharing
his own shadow with me. Inspired by his enthusiasm for
transformation and his willingness to be vulnerable, I feel ready for
my own journey of discovery, going into the dark to find the light.'
Tim Freke, author of Lucid Living and Soul Story

'Charlie Morley has written a fine book that brings a fresh and modern approach to working with the shadow. He has created a pathway to integrate the shadow in a down-to-earth and yet inspiring way, led by his own walking-his-talk approach to life. Charlie is the real deal. I wholeheartedly recommend this book.'
Ya'Acov Darling Khan, author of *Jaguar in the Body, Butterfly in the Heart*

'Dreaming Through Darkness *offers an incredible array of insights and an enlivening collection of exercises that help you to love the full spectrum of yourself and wake up to the most wonderful life.'*
Sandy C. Newbigging, author of *Mind Calm* and *Calm Cure*

'In this highly authentic and pioneering work, Charlie Morley shares his rich experience as one of the world's foremost lucid dreamers and offers tips on how every person can train to become lucid and aware of their shadows.'
Rob Nairn, author of *Living, Dreaming, Dying*

'I have always been fascinated by what the ancient Mexicans named the Cave: the place where our ancestral patterns, instincts, personal story and highest potential reside. This book has offered me new ways to work with my own Cave in order to be a better person. I really believe that the practices in this book could be life changing for many people.'
Sergio Magaña, author of *Caves of Power* and *The Toltec Secret*

'Morley surpasses discussion of dream yoga by inviting the inspired reader into the experience itself. To understand the pages ahead is to quicken the evolution of one's conscious awakening.'
Lama Choyin Rangdrol, author of *Black Buddha*

DREAMING
THROUGH
DARKNESS

DREAMING
THROUGH
DARKNESS

Shine Light into the Shadow to
Live the Life of Your Dreams

CHARLIE MORLEY

HAY
HOUSE

HAY HOUSE

Carlsbad, California • New York City • London
Sydney •Johannesburg • Vancouver • New Delhi

First published and distributed in the United Kingdom by:
Hay House UK Ltd, Astley House, 33 Notting Hill Gate, London W11 3JQ
Tel: +44 (0)20 3675 2450; Fax: +44 (0)20 3675 2451; www.hayhouse.co.uk

Published and distributed in the United States of America by:
Hay House Inc., PO Box 5100, Carlsbad, CA 92018-5100
Tel: (1) 760 431 7695 or (800) 654 5126; Fax: (1) 760 431 6948 or (800) 650 5115
www.hayhouse.com

Published and distributed in Australia by:
Hay House Australia Ltd, 18/36 Ralph St, Alexandria NSW 2015
Tel: (61) 2 9669 4299; Fax: (61) 2 9669 4144
www.hayhouse.com.au

Published and distributed in the Republic of South Africa by:
Hay House SA (Pty) Ltd, PO Box 990, Witkoppen 2068
info@hayhouse.co.za; www.hayhouse.co.za

Published and distributed in India by:
Hay House Publishers India, Muskaan Complex, Plot No.3, B-2,
Vasant Kunj, New Delhi 110 070
Tel: (91) 11 4176 1620; Fax: (91) 11 4176 1630; www.hayhouse.co.in

Distributed in Canada by:
Raincoast Books, 2440 Viking Way, Richmond, B.C. V6V 1N2
Tel: (1) 604 448 7100; Fax: (1) 604 270 7161; www.raincoast.com

A catalogue record for this book is available from the British Library.

ISBN: 978-1-78180-735-4

Interior illustrations: Liron Gilenberg | www.ironicitalics.com

Printed and bound by CPI Group (UK) Ltd, Croydon, CR0 4YY

To Rob Nairn
for lighting my way to the shadow

CONTENTS

LIST OF EXERCISES

FOREWORD

*Healing your shadow is the greatest gift
you can give yourself, your family,
your friends, your partner, the world.*

Before I sat down to write this Foreword I phoned Charlie to congratulate and thank him for writing this most illuminating book, *Dreaming through Darkness*. It's my honour to have been a mentor to Charlie for his inquiry on meeting, befriending and transmuting the shadow. From the outset, I encouraged Charlie to make every sentence he wrote as honest and truthful as possible. He did just that, and it's one reason why I found his book to be so healing and liberating.

I gave my first talk on shadow psychology in the winter of 1998, around the time of the solstice and many other festivals of light. I was speaking to students of The Interfaith Seminary, in the UK. The next year, I returned to give a one-day workshop on shadow psychology. The year after that, I gave a two-day workshop. This is how my teaching work on the shadow began. I've been teaching shadow psychology in one form or another ever since.

Perhaps it's inevitable that I would end up teaching shadow psychology. When I was nine years old, my family moved home to a small, modern bungalow called Shadows. Before that, we lived in a pretty little cottage called Honeysuckle Cottage. Who on earth, in their right mind, would move from Honeysuckle Cottage to Shadows, I ask you!

It was during my years living in Shadows that my world fell apart. My mother's recurring bouts of depression took a turn for the worse. Several times she was incarcerated in mental hospitals, plied with experimental drugs and subjected to brutal electric shock therapy. She did so well to get out alive. At the same time, my father's alcoholism got out of control. Eventually, he left home and he lived homeless on and off for the last 10 years of his life.

My parents' shadows became the catalyst for my interest in psychology and spirituality. My mum was so beautiful and funny; and my father was my hero. How could they not see it? Like Charlie did in his 20s, I explored the different faiths, schools of philosophy, Eastern and Western psychology, and the work of Carl Jung. Charlie has, from his own exploration, inserted precious gems of wisdom on every page of this book for you.

What is the shadow? Charlie sheds much light on this question. Where there is love, there is no shadow. Why? Love does not have an opposite. Love only ever attracts love. When you withhold love from yourself and others, for whatever reason, it casts a shadow. This shadow is a type of dream. It's not real because, unlike love, it won't last forever. Shadows fade and eventually disappear when you meet them with love. Charlie presents many effective ways for us to do this.

Charlie teaches us that there are two types of shadow. The dark shadow is made of self-judgements and a lack of self-acceptance. These are your unloveable bits and pieces, and typically include fear, pride, envy, competitiveness, grievances and anger, for example. The golden shadow is obscured by self-judgements and a lack of self-acceptance. It includes soul gifts, talents and positive qualities encoded in your spiritual DNA. Here, in the golden shadow, resides the artist, the teacher and the leader who you might not have met yet.

Charlie is best known for his work on lucid dreaming, and In *Dreaming through Darkness* he shares some classic lucid dreaming exercises. But that's not all. Charlie also presents a broad range of spiritual practices — all personally road-tested — to help you shine love on your shadow both at night and during the day. That's why I consider this book to be Charlie's breakthrough book, because herein he reveals more of his full repertoire as a spiritual teacher.

Shadow work takes courage. With Charlie as your guide and mentor, you are in good hands. Charlie knows how to be light and deep. It's a quality of one who knows how to befriend his or her shadow. He'll help you to be honest and positive. He'll show you the moves you need to dance with your shadow and guide you back to the astonishing light of your true being.

The gifts of shadow work are many. Befriending your shadow is, essentially, a path of self-forgiveness. Self-forgiveness leads you to the miracle of self-acceptance. The miracle is that when you're willing to love yourself, you emerge from the shadows and step into the present. There are no shadows in the present moment. Here is where you can honour your past and heal your future. Here and now you can step forwards as both a lightworker — and a shadow worker — who helps our world evolve in the direction of love.

Robert Holden
Author of *Shift Happens!* and *Loveability*
London, April 2017

INTRODUCTION

*'Out beyond ideas of wrongdoing
and rightdoing there is a field.
I'll meet you there.'*

Rumi[1]

Almost 10 years ago I was introduced to an approach to psychological growth that changed my view on life forever. This approach, and the practices it offered, gave me more confidence, more authenticity and access to a vast source of energy, both physical and mental, which I found within myself. It was called shadow integration.

The shadow is the part of us that is made up of all that we hide from others: our shame, our fears and our wounds, but also our divine spirit, our blinding beauty and our hidden talents.

Shadow integration involves shining light into the dark caves of our dreaming and waking minds to reveal the gold that is stored there. As I did the practices, I began to realize something: I had been looking for my gold in all the wrong places. Our true power is found not in the saccharine sweetness of 'spiritual bypassing' – overlooking our unenlightened human condition – but in the dazzling darkness of our unconscious mind. The light that we will find there is brighter than we can ever imagine.

This book will guide you into the unseen darkness of the shadow and show you how to uncover the gold hidden within. We will use ancient methods from Tibetan Buddhism alongside contemporary techniques from Western psychology to power this alchemical process. Every exercise has earned its place in this book and has been developed, tested and refined through the workshops that I have taught in over 20 countries around the world.

In Part I: Meeting the Shadow, we'll be laying the groundwork and exploring what the shadow is, the benefits of integrating it and how it appears in our dreams, as well as how we create and project it.

In Part II: Befriending the Shadow, we'll start to move deeper into the subject with the aspiration of making a friend and ally of our shadow side. We'll explore the masks that we wear, the 'no mud, no lotus' approach and learn how to revolutionize our view of nightmares and embrace our shadow through lucid dreaming.

And finally, in Part III: Transmuting the Shadow, we'll engage in a set of practices that can be truly life-changing: looking into our ancestral past, integrating our sexual story, transforming our inner demons and facing what for many of us is the ultimate shadow: fear of death and dying.

I've spent the past two years researching and writing about the shadow, and one of my guides through this process has been psychologist Robert Holden, a brilliant man who is often described as 'Britain's foremost expert on happiness'. Very early on in the writing process, Robert gave me some sound advice. He said, 'Don't try to write a bestselling book, or even a good book. Write a true book.'

So I set out to reveal the truth of my own shadow, fully and authentically, as a way of inspiring others to do the same. In using my own stories of shadow integration, I have exposed some of my most seemingly 'shameful' shadow aspects, a few of which may shock some of my more conservative readers. I don't seek to make excuses for these revelations – in fact, I believe it is vital that I unmask myself fully if I am to ask you to do the same.

So, be prepared. I will encourage you to move into places that may shock and scare you. You may be shocked by the brilliance of your divine light and scared by the responsibility that comes with this light, for once you've seen how much brilliance you contain, how can you possibly go on living the way you have been?

In fact, this book aims to empower you to change the way you live and change the way you dream – forever. Just as a single candle can illuminate a cave that has been dark for millennia, so these practices will bring radical illumination to your unseen potential.

Simply the act of reading this book is a peace offering to the shadow, an extended hand of friendship that (however tentatively) says, 'I am ready to know you.' With this gesture of love, we move into the freedom of shamelessness, the place beyond duality, beyond right and wrong, the place of Rumi's field.

I'll meet you there.

Charlie Morley
Kagyu Samye Dzong Buddhist Centre, London
February 2017

PART I

MEETING
THE SHADOW

'Loving oneself is no easy matter because it means loving all of oneself, including the shadow.'

JAMES HILLMAN[1]

There is a source of energy within us that contains the seed of awakening. We may hide it from others, though we know that it's there. Like fire, if ignored or misused, it may burn us, but if harnessed, it can warm us, protect us and revolutionize our life. We call it 'the shadow'.

CHAPTER 1

OUR DARK AND GOLDEN SHADOWS

'To own one's shadow is the purpose of life.
A full-bodied embracing of our own humanity.'

Robert A. Johnson[1]

The concept of the shadow is found within almost every culture and spiritual tradition the world over, but it was first popularized in the West by the legendary Swiss psychiatrist Carl Jung.* He used it to describe the part of the unconscious mind that was made up of all the seemingly undesirable aspects of the psyche.

The shadow is our dark side, but not dark as in 'negative' or 'malign', rather dark as in 'not yet illuminated'. It is comprised of everything within us that we don't want to face. That is, everything both seemingly harmful *and* potentially enlightening – all that we have rejected, denied, disowned or repressed.

So, the shadow is not evil or bad, it is simply the parts of ourselves that seem incompatible with who we think we are. These might include our shame, our fears, our emotional wounds and also, crucially, our awakened essence, our unexpressed talents and our highest potential.

---

* Jung, born in 1875, founded analytical psychology. As well as a ground-breaking psychiatrist, he was also a writer, artist and mystic, whose work explored myth, religion, anthropology and spirituality. He continued writing and creating right up until his death in 1961.

While writing this book I've come across dozens of different definitions of the shadow. From psychologists to shamans, everyone has their unique take on it. Psychologist Stephen Diamond sees it as 'all that we deem unacceptable and deny in ourselves'.[2] Shamanic practitioner Ya'Acov Darling Khan says it is 'anywhere that your fear becomes greater than your current capacity for love'.[3] Buddhist meditation teacher Rob Nairn calls it 'all the aspects of ourselves that we don't want to face'.[4]

The shadow is a wide-ranging term, but in this book we'll use it to refer to anything within us that we are unwilling to either accept or extend our love to.

The shadow is a creative powerhouse of untapped energy, so becoming aware of its contents and transmuting its power are hugely beneficial to our psycho-spiritual growth. Although different traditions refer to it in different terms, any spiritual path that aspires to psychological wholeness will incorporate shadow integration to some degree, simply because unless the shadow is integrated, the mind remains divided.

The Dark Shadow

Many people, when they first hear about the shadow, immediately think about their potentially harmful traits like anger, prejudice or hatred, or what might be considered unacceptable, such as sexual taboos. Interestingly, though, the shadow contains just as many – if not more – overtly beneficial traits such as inner strength, blinding beauty and talents that have been kept hidden. So it has two sides: dark and golden.

The dark shadow contains the rejected traits that we deem to be negative or harmful, such as anger, fear and shame. It contains the answers to questions like 'What am I most afraid of?', 'What am I most ashamed of?' and 'What do I hide from others?'

The shadow is often misinterpreted as something bad or harmful, which leads us to waste the valuable integration process it offers by investing energy in either denying it or trying to defeat it. The truth is, though, that the shadow is neither bad nor harmful; it is simply unintegrated energy, and until we learn how to tap into this energy and transmute its power, we will never become a fully integrated or fully awakened human being.

The poet Rainer Maria Rilke said, 'Perhaps everything terrible is, in its deepest essence, something helpless that wants our love,'[5] and so it is with the shadow. Becoming a shadow worker, as you will see, is all about love.

The Golden Shadow

The golden shadow (often called the positive* shadow) is made up of our hidden talents, our blinding beauty and our unfulfilled potential. It contains our intuition, our creativity, childlike vitality and spiritual power. Just as the dark shadow is made up of all the parts of ourselves that we fear may lead to rejection, the golden shadow is made up of all the bright, brilliant and magnificent parts of ourselves that we fear may be too great, too awesome or too challenging to reveal to ourselves and others.

The golden shadow is our unactivated potential, our unused talents, and just as it takes conscious effort to reclaim and transform the energy stored in our dark shadow, so must we make an effort to reclaim the golden shadow's energy if we are to be complete, balanced and authentically whole.

Jungian author Robert A. Johnson has said that to be willing to draw the skeletons out of the closet is quite easy, but to truly own the gold in the shadow can be much more difficult. This is because the golden shadow challenges our self-image.

---

* I have found the duality of the words 'positive' and 'negative' to be unhelpful when referring to the shadow, so I will use the terms 'golden shadow' and 'dark shadow' from now on.

Truly owning our highest potential and waking up to the infinite brightness of our inner light is such a threat to who we think we are that our limiting ego-mind will often do everything it can to prevent us from doing so.

Where do you hide your light or limit yourself? What golden traits are you unwilling to love? Is it your esoteric side that you hide from others for fear of being labelled too 'woo-woo'? (I believe that's the technical term for it.) Or is it your natural sexuality that you shy away from for fear of being labelled as 'shameful' or 'too glamorous'?* Is it your innate intelligence that you temper for fear of seeming 'too clever'? Or perhaps it's the bright light of your spiritual potential that you daren't explore for fear that it might isolate you from your friends or family?

Many of us hold the unconscious belief that our golden shadow traits may lead to jealousy, suspicion or rejection if revealed. But, as Marianne Williamson famously said, 'There is nothing enlightened about shrinking so that other people won't feel insecure around you. We are all meant to shine, as children do.'[6] To own our golden shadow is to allow ourselves to shine.

Dark or Golden?

The dark and golden shadows are, in fact, different parts and often polar opposites of the same thing. David Richo, in his brilliant book *Shadow Dance*, describes the dark shadow as 'a cellar of our unexamined shame' and the golden shadow as 'an attic of our unclaimed valuables'.[7]

It's only our self-judgement and societal belief systems that make shadow content fall into one category or the other. In some cultures 'vivacious individuality' would be classed as a

---

* The ancient Celts used to have a word for the tangible presence of a woman's feminine power and vitality; that word was 'glamour'.

dark shadow, whereas in others it would be classed as golden. The specific culture into which we are born may insist that we behave in a particular manner, obliging us to separate out all our unacceptable traits if we are to be accepted by the tribe. It's interesting to note that it is essentially differences in shadow content between one culture and another that so often contribute to conflict and strife on a worldwide scale.

The Shadow of the World

Although this book is primarily focused around integration of the personal shadow, it's important at least to address the concept of the collective shadow.

Carl Jung spoke not only of a personal unconscious, the aspects of our own mind of which we are unaware, but also of a collective unconscious: a vast storehouse of ancient human experience, containing themes and images found cross-culturally throughout history. It is a kind of transpersonal library of the universal history and inherited experience of all humankind, and it also has a shadow.

The collective shadow is made up of the dark side of society 'fed by neglected and repressed collective values'[8] such as racism, taboos and tribally dualistic mindsets. It also holds the repressed fear-based shadows of the world: war, environmental destruction, human and animal holocausts, and the shadow of our refusal to accept responsibility for integrating these.

The personal shadow is the bridge to the global one, so becoming aware of our own shadow keeps us from 'falling into the mass psychosis of the collective shadow'.[9] When we integrate our own shadow, we not only contribute less to the projected chaos of blame, shame and pain in which many human relationships occur, but we also add less to the collective shadow, which fosters conflict on a wider scale.

So, the more people who integrate their shadow, the better for the world at large. By shining light into your own unilluminated shadows you help light the way for others. As meditation master Lama Yeshe Rinpoche* says, 'To tame ourselves is the only way to change the world.'[10]

Shadow work really can change the world and contribute to a more harmonious society. We are all interdependently linked to millions of other people, and so every change we make, every shadow we integrate, will undoubtedly impact upon the wider world.

Let's look at shadow integration a bit more closely.

What Is Shadow Integration?

Shadow integration can be seen as a process that enables unconscious psychological material to be recognized and accepted by the conscious mind, thus resulting in the beneficial release of that psychological energy into the wholeness of the psyche.

But what does that actually mean?

It means that we can transmute the unseen power of the shadow into the energy of awakening. This is the purpose of every exercise in this book.

Anytime we move from shame to loving acceptance, we integrate a shadow aspect. Anytime we transform a fear or make friends with anxiety, we integrate a shadow aspect. Anytime we are courageous enough to accept (not condone, but accept) the most shameful parts of ourselves, anytime we choose love over fear and anytime we step into the fullest expression of who we are, we integrate our shadow.

---

* 'Lama' is a title usually given to a person who has done at least one three-year Tibetan Buddhist retreat. *Rinpoche* is a Tibetan word meaning 'precious' (pronounced with an accent on the 'e' so that it rhymes with the word 'cabaret') and is an honorific title given to meditation masters in Tibetan Buddhism.

By consciously illuminating and befriending our shadow material, we release the energy that it contains, lighten the load of our shame and manifest our highest potential. To look into our dazzling darkness and embrace our shadow with love is to move into the fullest expression of ourselves.

It is crucial to remember that shadow integration is *not* about getting rid of the shadow. We want to harness its energy, not destroy it. And yet our aim is not to act it out or indulge it either. This will simply solidify its separation from us. Instead, we want to befriend it and transmute its energy into benevolent power.

This radical approach to dealing with the dark side is not new. For over 1,000 years, practitioners of Tibetan Buddhism and other mystical traditions have been intentionally confronting the forces of 'fear, aggression and desire so that the practitioner can channel them into the creative expression'[11] of spiritual awakening. Full integration of our shadow is integral to full enlightenment.

The end goal is to know ourselves[12] and to witness where everything within us lies, both the best and the worst of us. We then make friends with those parts and harness the energy that they hold to fuel the fire of spiritual transformation.

Shadow Dreaming

If you want to know your shadow, it helps to know your dreams.

The themes, characters and symbols of our dreams are often used by our unconscious mind to highlight areas of ourselves of which we are unaware and which require integration. Shadow material forms a large part of this.

When we dream, the shadow, both dark and golden, can be displayed openly and without the censorship of the waking mind. So if we open up to our dreams, we are opening up to the shadow.

Our shadow actually *wants* to be known and so it will display itself in our dreams in the hope that we will recognize it, because through that simple act of recognition it will begin to be integrated.

Dreaming of themes related to our shadow is actually a very good sign, but when the dark shadow displays itself at maximum volume, we may label the experience a nightmare and in our aversion miss the opportunity to recognize and integrate it. (In Chapter 8 we will start to reframe this aversion.)

Throughout this book we'll be learning all the techniques we need to start remembering, recognizing and even directing our dreams. Through lucid dreaming (the art of becoming fully conscious within our dreams), we'll be able to invoke our shadow, dialogue with it in personified form and even embrace it as a way of transmuting its energy.

We'll devote two whole chapters to lucid dream shadow work and there are lucid dreaming techniques in an appendix at the back of this book, so don't worry if you don't know how to lucid dream yet. If you're wondering exactly what a lucid dream feels like, take a moment to have a look at some of the lucid dreams in Appendix II (see *page 235*).

Lucid Living: Live the Life of Your Dreams?

If lucid dreaming is about becoming fully conscious in our dreams, then lucid living is about becoming more conscious in the shared dream of waking life.

Most of us live as we dream: in the shadowy darkness of non-awareness. So much of our life is lived this way: we sleepwalk through relationships, are too tired to activate our potential and make crucial life choices with sleep in our eyes. Lucid living is about taking charge of our waking life in much the same way as we take charge of our lucid dreams. As we take back the reins of our life and live more lucidly, we embrace the shadow elements of daily life fearlessly and work through psychological blocks more creatively. Shadow work is the ultimate lucid living practice in that it asks us to wake up and become conscious to everything within us that we have been denying and rejecting.

The practices in this book encourage us to wake up and to start dreaming *through* the darkness and into the bright light of our fully lucid state. Essentially, every time we embrace a shadow aspect in our dreams, we are planting seeds to do the same in our waking life.

Through this, we open up the possibility of quite literally *living the life of our dreams*, for as we learn to become lucid at night, we find our level of dream awareness being reflected in our waking life too. And with that we begin to dream our life into existence.

***

Now that we've covered the basics of what the shadow is and touched on how shadow integration works, let's take a look at some of the benefits of shadow integration.

CHAPTER 2

THE BENEFITS OF SHADOW INTEGRATION

*'The truth of the matter is that the shadow
is ninety percent pure gold.'*

C.G. Jung[1]

This book is going to ask you to move into places you may never have been before and never dreamed of going. It will ask you to explore your fear, retrace your life story, integrate your sexual shadow, face your own mortality and step into your highest potential. Shadow work takes effort, but the benefits can be life-changing, so let's explore a few of the key ones now.

Key Benefits

Increased Energy

The shadow is one of the most powerful energy sources in the human mind and yet for many of us it becomes an energetic drain, because we waste so much energy trying to deny or destroy it. Think how much energy you invest in keeping your shadow side hidden. Imagine what life could be like if you could release and harness that energy...

Shadow integration does exactly that. We don't get rid of the shadow, we simply regain the energy we have been using to suppress it. This allows us to move back into our natural human condition, which is one of boundless energy, energy the ancient Greeks called *enthousiasmós*, meaning 'possessed by the gods', which these days we call 'enthusiasm'.

How does this newly integrated energy actually manifest? We experience it both as literally more physical energy and more subtly as an increase in the energy flow often called *chi* or *prana*. This increase in psychic energy may be subtle at first, but it may become quite tangible once we begin the transmutation practices and the proverbial weight on our shoulders is released.

A man on one of my shadow courses who works as an energy healer told me: 'I feel as though I'm firing on all cylinders. I feel lighter, but more energized too. Something's definitely working here!' This was a textbook example of someone feeling the energizing effects of shadow integration.

Individuation

Individuation has been described as the process by which we 'fulfil our potential and become all that we can be'.[2] It is a Jungian term that refers to full psychological completeness and self-actualization. It's been said that it is how every person becomes who they are destined to become. Crucially, though, it is dependent upon the integration of the shadow.

Jung himself was unequivocal on this. He said that we had to confront the shadow, that there was no other choice.

If we don't integrate our shadow, we may tend to have weaker or shallower psyches. That doesn't mean that we are weak or shallow people, simply that our psychological depth will be limited by the depth to which we have ventured into it.

It is only by showing love to our unloved shadow aspects that we can reach the full psychological completeness of individuation.

Increased Love and Compassion

One of the most profound things I ever heard meditation teacher Rob Nairn say was: 'The most compassionate thing you can do is to be yourself. In all your wonderfully neurotic messiness, just be yourself.'

Compassion is not an activity we choose to do, it is a quality of being, a state of mind and a mode of communication that aspires to see the Buddha beneath the bullshit in every person that we meet, including ourselves.

Meeting and befriending our own unilluminated dark side is not only the most compassionate thing we can offer ourselves, it is also the best method for working compassionately with the shadow sides of other people. Through opening up to our own pain and shame, we become more empathetic to that of others, and our hearts become expanded with mercy.

It's been said that 'the shadow is the bridge to universal compassion'.[3] And with compassion comes courage – the courage to shine light into the areas of our mind that we dare not look into. Courage is, in fact, integral to the application of compassion,[4] because compassion, for both ourselves and others, is an act of true bravery.

We must not confuse compassion with approval, however. To do so may limit the free expression of our compassion, as we wait to pass approval before offering it. We need not approve of what we show love to, but just be willing to love it regardless.

Amplified Creativity

Carl Jung famously said that in spite of it acting as a reservoir for human darkness, the shadow was also the seat of all creativity.

Most of our creative energy is stored in the shadow, in large part, as we will explore in Chapter 12, due to the suppression of sexual energy that most of us unconsciously partake in. When we liberate the energy tied up in the shadow, this creative energy will automatically be released into the conscious mind, leading to amplified creativity in all forms.

This creative juice may be experienced as an almost libidinal energy by some, but although creative energy and sexual energy are linked (what could be more creative than the sexual act?), this does not mean that it will express itself in a sexualized form.

However, our creative life-force energy (sometimes called *chi* or *prana*) will start to flow more readily and this may express itself in a kind of *bounce* or *uplift* within our creative centres, as new ideas, creative problem-solving abilities and artistic inspiration start to emerge.

Spiritual Growth

Shadow work also produces a more mature personality and leads directly to spiritual growth. Our spiritual development is actually dependent upon the degree to which we have integrated our shadow. Full shadow integration, both dark and golden, is not simply a prerequisite for awakening, it is synonymous with it.

Imagine a steam train pottering through the countryside. As it moves along the tracks over the flat ground, it can get all the power it needs from just a few shovelfuls of coal. Now imagine the steam train making its way up a steep mountain track. It will naturally require loads more coal to power it up the mountain. If we want to make it to the mountaintop, we need more energy, and that means going into the shadow. It is the only way.

Not everyone agrees with this, though. Some people feel that 'being spiritual' is about smiling all the time and denying our dark shadow for fear of 'manifesting negativity'. This tendency to overlook or minimize our unenlightened human condition is called 'spiritual bypassing' and leads to stunted spiritual growth.

Without harnessing the power and life-force stored in the shadow, we can only go so far on the spiritual path, but if we can learn to transmute the energy of the shadow into the gold of awakening, there are no limits to how far we can go.

Optimized Health

Shadow work may help maintain our physical health too. Within the Tibetan Buddhist teachings it's said that 'to feel psychologically, emotionally and spiritually whole is both the greatest source of healing and the strongest protection against illness',[5] and with so many physical illnesses being either partially caused by or at least exacerbated by emotional imbalance, I'm sure most of us would agree with that.

Western science agrees too, as studies have shown that improving the balance and integration of our mind can lead to our body moving to a more balanced and optimized level of health. A University of Toronto study shows that holding past trauma, shame, fear and especially prejudice can be linked to chronic problems like cancer, hypertension and Type 2 diabetes,[6] and so any interventions we can make to integrate our shadows of fear and prejudice will help reduce these problems.

Unsurprisingly, integrating our golden shadow is also great for our health. Scientific studies have shown that the symptoms of golden shadow integration such as 'increased happiness, hopefulness, optimism and contentment have been shown to reduce the risk and limit the severity of cardiovascular disease, diabetes, hypertension and respiratory infections'[7] – clinical evidence that embracing your golden shadow is good for you.

Authenticity

For me, one of the greatest benefits of shadow work is authenticity. I've been exploring the shadow for over a decade now and for the past few years shadow work has become one of my main spiritual practices. So, do I now have a fully integrated shadow? Absolutely not. Have I faced and embraced all my demons? Not a chance. (I had no idea I had so many till I started this work!) So, what has shadow work done for me? It's made me a hell of a lot more authentic.

At the end of 2015, I began a three-month Buddhist meditation retreat. During that time I was mostly alone, mostly in silence and mostly meditating all day. I discovered that when you do nothing but meditate all day, the shadow can be abundantly and quite shockingly revealed.

As the days turned to weeks, I came face to face with my dark shadow: the part of me that was a judgemental, neurotic control freak with addictive tendencies and an impostor syndrome. I witnessed what I came to refer to as my 'Magnificent Messiness'. I became aware of the jealous, angry, perverted and shameful parts of myself that I had denied and rejected for years in the hope of being a 'good Buddhist' – whatever that means.

The more I looked, the more I saw, but strangely, the more I saw, the lighter I started to feel, as if simply witnessing those denied aspects of myself relaxed the tension they had been causing in my mind and released the weight of their burden. I soon started to feel more confident, more real, more authentically myself.

And I saw the other side of myself too: my golden shadow, the part of me that was so brilliant and so bright that it was just as hard to look at. I saw that this blinding light is in all living beings, innately, simply as a by-product of the miracle of being alive.

By the end of three months, I realized that shadow work was not about fixing yourself or becoming 'good', it was about making friends with your mind, learning to love yourself and showing up authentically, as a beautifully imperfect human being, and embracing your Magnificent Messiness.

***

Throughout this book, if ever you're struggling with an exercise, can't be bothered anymore or just forget why you wanted to work with your shadow in the first place, please come back to this list of benefits to remind yourself of just how beneficial this work is for your psychological and spiritual growth.

Fear of the Shadow?

At the shadow workshops I run, even after hearing about all of these benefits some people still feel a bit scared about approaching their dark shadow and a few even worry whether it's safe to do so.

It's totally natural to feel a bit of fear around shadow work (fear is actually one of the building blocks of our shadow), but in fact, integrating the shadow is the safest thing we will ever do.

The common approach to dealing with seemingly 'negative' emotions is to judge them, deny them and hide them from the world and from ourselves. This approach is unwise, though, because if we shove them into the recesses of our mind, they gather, gain power over us and occasionally erupt, or spill forth when our guard is dropped. Sharing our headspace with an unseen and unloved shadow side is a recipe for agitation, anxiety and self-sabotage.

Jung said that the less conscious of our shadow we were, the darker and denser it would be. So to be conscious of our shadow, to know it and show loving acceptance to it, is the greatest and safest gift we can ever give ourselves.

The longer things stay in the shadows, the darker and denser they become, and yet once we're ready to shine light into the places that scare us, we can unravel decades of darkness in one moment of clarity. The shape of this book will help you shine that light in a safe and contained way by gradually introducing you to your shadow. Follow the exercises step by step and take it as slowly as you need to.

The shadow wants to be known and the mind wants to be integrated – that is a natural inbuilt function* – and they will only show you what you are ready for, no more.

So you have a choice: either learn to befriend the shadow consciously or allow it to express itself unconsciously through some neurosis, habitual pattern or unbeneficial behaviour.

If you are new to shadow work then you have almost certainly been doing the latter since childhood, so, if for no other reason than curiosity, why not try this new approach? You've nothing to lose but your limits.

Intention and Motivation

You are about to engage in the first of the practical exercises, which will bring you to a direct meeting with your shadow. This requires looking at your dark side. This isn't 'dark' as in 'bad', remember, rather 'dark' as in 'unilluminated'. Nonetheless, this is a side of ourselves that most of us prefer not to look at, and exploring it can be prickly work. It's like exploring a rose bush – you will find great beauty, but occasionally you may encounter a thorn. So, please go slowly, be gentle with yourself and maintain a sense of playfulness.

---

* In psychological terms Jung described this as an intelligent self-regulation mechanism in the psyche that strives to maintain balance within the mind.

As you do the exercises, especially some of the ones in Part III, be sure to talk through your experiences whenever you need to with a trusted friend, therapist or coach.

Before you start, though, as with anything else that you do, it makes sense to ask yourself, 'What do I intend to do?' and 'Why do I want to do it?'

If you're reading this book, it's probably safe to say that what you intend to do is to learn and practise shadow integration, but why do you want to do it? To further your spiritual growth or to be more authentic? To reclaim your shadow energy or to step into your highest potential?

Whatever your reasons, take a moment now to set your intention and motivation. It'll only take two minutes.

Exercise: Setting Your Intention and Motivation

Step 1
Begin by *expanding your mindful awareness*. This sounds like a big deal, but actually it can be quite easy to do.

- Sitting with a straight back and with your eyes open or closed (either is fine), breathing through your nose or mouth (either is fine), come to an awareness of your breath. Just notice when you are breathing in and when you are breathing out. As you breathe in, you might notice *I'm breathing in, my body is expanding slightly,* and then as you breathe out, you might notice *I'm breathing out and my body is releasing and relaxing*.

- Notice with awareness three more inhalations and exhalations.

Step 2
- Now, allowing your breath to return to its natural flow, take a moment to become aware of your body.

- Simply notice the contact points of your body with the chair or surface beneath you.

- Then expand your awareness to your bodily sensations, particularly to any areas of tension. You can imagine releasing these as you relax into the out-breath.

Step 3

- Now release your focus on bodily sensations and allow yourself to rest. Just sit there.

- In this state of rest, ask yourself: 'Why do I want to explore my shadow?' Simply drop the question like a pebble into water and watch the ripples. Maybe a direct answer will arise or maybe not. Either is fine. The most important thing is that you have asked the question.

Feel free to go through the Intention-and-Motivation-setting process before every or any of the exercises in this book.

Exercise: Meeting Aspects of Your Shadow

Now that you've set your intention and motivation, you're ready to explore some of what makes up your personal shadow, both the dark and golden aspects.

The questions below are a way of just gently dipping your toes into some of your personal shadow content. Whatever you find there, remember that your shadow is the part of you that is yet to be loved, so love, rather than judgement, is what you need to integrate it.

This exercise uses two sets of questions (inspired by a similar exercise in Debbie Ford's *Dark Side of the Light Chasers*) to help you tune in to the unique aspects of your personal shadow. The first set will help you meet some aspects of your dark shadow.

Step 1

- Take a moment to come into an awareness of your breath. Just notice when you are breathing in and notice when you are breathing out.

- Notice with awareness three inhalations and exhalations before you begin. This will help to settle your mind.

Step 2

- Answer the following questions without too much deliberation – the first answer that comes is often the truest, but feel free to have several answers for each question. Note your answers down if possible.

  - 'What am I most afraid of?'

  - 'What lies about myself do I tell others?'

  - 'What am I most ashamed of?'

  - 'What do I hide from others?'

  - 'What personal habits cause me pain?'

  - 'What part of my body am I least happy with?'

  - 'If I can remember, what are the themes of my anxiety dreams or nightmares?'

Step 3

- Make a list of the key points from your answers to the questions above, entitled 'Aspects of My Dark Shadow'.

  You may end up with a list that looks something like mine:

Aspects of My Dark Shadow
Failure/exposure
That I'm stronger than I am/better than I am/gentler than I am
My past habits/the way I used to be
My past/my loneliness/knowledge/sexuality
Judgemental thinking/guilt complex/impostor syndrome
Skinny legs
Losing control/zombies

Step 4

- Read through your list and take a moment to consider how each answer makes you feel.

Remind yourself that your shadow isn't bad, it's simply the parts of yourself that you are unwilling to love and that everything on your list, however seemingly harmful, will have a helpful element within it.

Step 5

- Find a way to send loving acceptance to your list of shadow traits. You might like to say, either out loud or in your mind, 'I see you, my shadow,' to each aspect on your list.

  The shadow wants to be known, so once you let a shadow trait know that you see it, it may well stop displaying itself so loudly.

Now here are some questions to help you meet some aspects of your golden shadow.

Step 1

- Take a moment to come into an awareness of your breath. Just notice when you are breathing in and notice when you are breathing out.

- Notice with awareness three inhalations and exhalations before you begin.

Step 2

- Answer the following questions without too much deliberation – the first answer that comes is often the truest, but feel free to have several answers for each question. Note your answers down if possible.

  - 'What things in life bring out the best in me?'
  - 'If I didn't need money and were "following my bliss"* how would I spend my life?'
  - 'Based on a playful amplification of my own personality, if I had one superpower, what would it be?'
  - 'What things in life make my heart sing?'
  - 'In what areas of life do I hide my light?'
  - 'What do I want to be when I grow up?'

---

*   The esteemed mythologist Joseph Campbell believed that 'following your bliss' meant identifying the pursuit that you were truly passionate about and attempting to give yourself absolutely to it. In so doing, you would achieve your fullest potential and serve your community to the greatest possible extent.

Step 3

- Make a list of the key points from your answers to the questions above, entitled 'Aspects of My Golden Shadow'.

  You may end up with a list that looks something like mine:

Aspects of My Golden Shadow

Practising Buddhism/teaching/helping others
Teaching/learning/mind expansion
Infinite enthusiasm!
Loved ones/bringing joy/dancing/play
Spiritual stuff
Enlightened (or a rock star)

Step 4

- Read through your list and remind yourself that your golden shadow is simply the parts of yourself that you are yet to fully activate.

- Find a way to ask for the activation of your golden shadow traits. You might like to use an affirmation such as:

  I see you, my golden shadow, and I activate your potential.

Step 5

- Take a moment to dedicate the beneficial energy of this exercise to yourself and to all living beings, using the statement:

  I dedicate the beneficial energy generated by this exercise to the benefit of all beings.

Now that you're aware of some of the aspects of your personal shadow, you might be thinking, *What do I do now? Did I do it right?* As Zen master Thich Nhat Hanh says, 'Awareness is like the sun. When it shines on things, they are naturally transformed.'[8] So at this point on your journey there's no need to do anything but be *aware* of these aspects.

In Your Dreams...

Many people find that shadow work has a noticeable effect on their dreams. You'll only notice this effect if you are in the habit of noticing your dreams, though, and so I'll be asking you to try to remember your dreams and to keep a dream diary throughout this process.

To be aware of your dreams is to be aware of your shadow. By recalling your dreams, you start to see the shadow on its own turf: the unconscious mind. With every dream, the unconscious mind (and the shadow content it contains) is offering you the hand of friendship. Remembering your dreams and acknowledging their value will enable you to take that hand.

But what, you may say, if you don't dream? The truth is that everybody dreams. Based on an average eight-hour sleep cycle, most people have four or five dream periods every night, but not everybody remembers them. Why? Often simply because they don't try to remember them. Most people find that with a little effort they can soon start to recall their dreams, though. Here's an exercise to help direct that effort.

Exercise: Boosting Dream Recall

If we set a strong intention to recall our dreams before we go to sleep each night, most of us will be able to recall at least part of them without too much difficulty. It often shocks people how easily they start remembering their dreams once they actually try to.

Five Steps to Boosting Your Dream Recall

1. Set your intention to recall your dreams before you start dreaming. Before bed and then as you're actually falling asleep, recite over and over in your mind:

    Tonight, I remember my dreams. I have excellent dream recall.

2. Try waking yourself briefly during a dream period, so that the dream is fresh in your mind. When do dream periods occur? Dreaming is part of every 90-minute cycle of sleep, but the last two hours of your sleep cycle are when your longest dream periods occur.

3. Often, dream memories are felt in the body rather than held in the mind, so don't forget to explore any bodily feelings that you wake up with. Sometimes dream recall can be as simple as:

    Can't remember much of the dream, but I woke
    with a feeling of happiness in my belly.

4. If you can recall just one image from a dream, you can work backwards from that point and eventually gather the rest of it. As soon as you wake up, ask yourself:

    Where was I? What was I just doing? How do I feel?

5. Don't give up if you can't remember a dream straight away. Give yourself the time and space to remember. The memory might not appear until hours after you've woken up. That's fine.

The most important of these five steps is the first one: set your intention to remember your dreams by mentally reciting, as you fall asleep,

Tonight, I remember my dreams. I have excellent dream recall.

If you do this every night for a week, you'll soon break even the strongest dream blackout.

If you haven't remembered a dream for years, then just recalling a tiny fragment is a great success, so work from where you are and don't put too much pressure on yourself to remember every dream straight away.

In the next chapter you'll learn how to keep a dream diary and then how to decode the shadow content from your dreams, but for now just focus on setting your intention to remember your dreams.

CHAPTER 3

CONSTRUCTING THE SHADOW

'Only when we're brave enough to explore the darkness will we discover the infinite power of our light.'

Brené Brown[1]

In both its forms, dark and golden, it's important to know that the shadow is a dynamic matrix of energy, which we are constantly either adding to or integrating. Within Jungian analytical psychology, it is classed as an *archetype*.

Archetypes can be understood as symbolic representations of universally existing aspects of the unconscious mind. They are themes of psychological energy, such as the Inner Child, the Wise Man and the Trickster, which seem to appear within every human mind in every part of the world.

Whereas all the other archetypes come pre-planted in the human psyche, the unique thing about the shadow is that it is self-constructed. That's good news, because it means that it can be deconstructed, too, and with that we can integrate its energy.

So how exactly do we construct our shadow? And why?

Suppression, Repression and Denial

Rob Nairn has lectured on both criminology and Tibetan Buddhism for over 40 years, so his particular take on the shadow is quite unique. When I asked him how we constructed our shadow, he said, 'The shadow is the accumulated effect of pushing away aspects of ourselves that we don't want to know about. It all comes down to suppression, repression and denial.'[2]

Let's have a closer look at these:

- *Suppression:* The process of consciously pushing away uncomfortable psychological material. For example, I feel depressed. I don't want to feel depressed, so I watch the entire boxset of *Game of Thrones* and eat a whole tube of Pringles. (Works every time.)

- *Repression:* The unconscious expulsion or 'forgetting' of distressing memories, thoughts or feelings from the conscious mind. Basically, repression is like suppression, but it happens at an unconscious level, so you don't know you're doing it.

- *Denial:* A psychological defence mechanism in which the existence of unpleasant external realities is rejected and kept out of conscious awareness. Denial is similar to repression, but whereas repression relates to internal mental material, denial relates primarily to external situations. For example, I deny that my wife is cheating on me even when I find her in bed with another man.

Rob told me, 'Whenever we suppress a feeling or deny a part of ourselves, we create shadow, and as we go through life, we are doing this constantly. We unconsciously push away what we don't want to feel and what we think will harm us. These may be very small things – annoyances, upsets, emotional wounds, embarrassments and rejections.'

They may be small, but just as small drops fill a big bucket, soon we have a heavy reservoir of rejected psychological energy weighing us down, and to try to lighten the load we start to project it out onto others.

Luckily for us, though, through shadow integration practice, denial can become acknowledgement, suppression can become friendliness and repression can become remembering.

Shame, Fear and Judgement

If suppression, repression and denial are the mechanisms that construct the shadow, then the actual building blocks of it are primarily made up of shame, fear and judgement. Every time we shame ourselves or others, every time we turn away from what scares us and every time we judge ourselves or others, we create shadow material.

Shame

Shame, in its purest expression, is the feeling that what we have done is going to make us unworthy of love. Although often used interchangeably with guilt, shame is actually quite different. Guilt says, 'I've done something bad,' but shame says, 'I am bad.' Guilt, although not always the most helpful emotion, at least has an active component in that it allows us to apologize and change our future behaviour constructively, whereas shame is inactive, stagnant and its secrecy negates the opportunity for constructive change.

Guilt can keep us up at night, but shame can actually hurt us. A 2011 study funded by the National Institute of Mental Health found that from a neurological perspective, physical pain and intense experiences of shame hurt in the same way. The study revealed that there is neural overlap between the experience of painful sensations in the body and the experience of shame and rejection.[3]

In her book *Daring Greatly*, shame researcher Brené Brown, PhD, offers three main perspectives on shame, which can be summarized as:[4]

1. Everybody has it – it's a universal emotion.

2. We are all afraid to talk about it.

3. The less we talk about it, the more power it has over us.

Unspoken shame breeds fear: fear that what we have done makes us unlovable and fear of others discovering our shame. We fear that this will lead to the removal of their love and maybe even rejection from 'the tribe'. (In prehistoric times these two outcomes could be tantamount to death, which is why fear of being shamed is so hardwired within us.)

To counter this, many shadow integration practices involve acknowledging and talking about our shame. As Jungian analyst Gilda Frantz once said, 'Shame is the gristle we must chew to integrate the shadow complex.'[5]

Fear

Anything within us that we are afraid of or that we are afraid to look at forms part of our shadow. Shadow work is fundamentally about making friends with what scares us: our darkness, but also our light.

Every time we daren't look at our shame, our life is ruled by fear. Fear is what keeps us from the mountaintop, yet it is not lack of fear that gets us there, but courage. Courage is not a lack of fear, it is the willingness to make friends with it.

Fear is one of the greatest obstacles to living a fully engaged life and fear of our own shadow is fear that most of us carry. It creates dense energetic blocks in our psycho-physical system, which prevent our fullest golden potential from displaying itself.

Shining light into the places that frighten us forms the basis of shadow work.

Judgement

Judgement is based on separation. It requires the dualistic polarity of good and bad, self and other, like and dislike. Anything within ourselves that we judge 'unacceptable' or are unwilling to be one with will become separate from us. It is this process of separation that creates not only our shadow, but the majority of human suffering.

So much of our suffering can be traced to some kind of separation – separation from the one we love, from the life we wish we had, from the contentment that we desire to feel – and most happiness can be traced to some kind of union – union with another person, with God, with our highest potential. Shadow work is fundamentally about moving from separation to unification. This is done in part through lessening our habitual addiction to judging or blaming ourselves and others.

This doesn't mean that we give up discernment. Shadow work requires the wise discernment that can see what is harmful and what is helpful. It's not discernment that creates shadow, but the process of being judgemental.

Being less judgemental actually allows us to be *more* discerning as we learn to operate from a place of discerning wisdom rather than judgemental projection.

Projecting Our Shadow

'We do not see things as they are. We see things as we are.'
Rabbi Shmuel Ben Nachmani[6]

So far we have explored some of the building blocks of the shadow, but the actual dynamic energy that keeps the whole show on the road is projection. The shadow is created, sustained and revealed through psychological projection.

Projection can be defined as 'a psychological defence mechanism in which we unconsciously transpose our own unacceptable qualities onto others'. It is the main method of communication that the shadow uses to make itself known to us. One of the most direct ways of meeting our shadow is by seeing how we project it onto others.

Although we often project our unacceptable traits onto others, much of our projection is actually quite benign. Doesn't it seem as though more people in the street are smiling when you are in love?

Projection is, in many ways, how we connect with people: we project our energy outwards, this energy is picked up by others and they either reflect or solidify our projection. This all happens way before we've even said hello.

It's fascinating to watch. It's as if our fragile ego needs continuous reassurance of its existence and it gets it through a kind of echo-location: constantly projecting its energy outwards as a way of working out its place in the world.

Creating Reality

When I first started teaching lucid dreaming, I was still quite young and had a heavy dose of impostor syndrome. Once, while teaching at a Buddhist centre, I created an entire reality based on my projection of this.

As I started to teach the more complex side of Tibetan dream work, I saw a woman in the back row making strange facial expressions, grimacing even, each time I concluded a relevant point.

This grimacing went on throughout my talk. I wasn't confident about the subtleties of what I was teaching and soon my head was spinning: *I knew I shouldn't have tried to teach the complex stuff! This woman hates me! She obviously knows more about it than I do! I'm a fraud!*

At the tea break I decided to embrace my shadow and went straight over to talk to her.

To my surprise, before I could even introduce myself, she had burst into a warm, lopsided smile and said how much she had enjoyed the first session. Up close, it was clear that she had had a stroke and that when she smiled (at least from the back row), it looked a little bit like a grimace.

My apprehension around teaching the complex Tibetan stuff had been projected onto the audience, where it had latched onto a misconception of reality (grimacing in disapproval) that supported its perceived truth. Through projection, I had created an external reality that supported my internal one. And with that, I understood the words of the Buddha himself: 'With our minds we make the world.'

As this story shows, projection can be quite difficult to recognize when you're in the midst of it. So simply noticing it is a massive step forward in personal growth and vital to shadow integration.

Projection Reveals the Dark Shadow

We are sometimes so disconnected from our shadow side that we see it only in proxy, through reflection or projection.

Projection is a huge subject, so we are going to focus primarily on the three main types of dark shadow projection. Let's explore them one by one.

'It's You, Not Me'

The psychotherapist David Richo believes that: 'What strongly repels us in others is a clue to where our own darkness lurks.'[7]

He explains that the disliked features of our own personality are projected as repulsion and aversion towards those who demonstrate those very traits.

Essentially, what annoys us most in other people is often indicative of what we are unwilling to recognize and accept in ourselves. We often become overly sensitive to precisely these disowned traits.

From this perspective, annoyance is like the grit that agitates the clam to make the pearl. Without it, we would have no reference point as to where our dark shadow lies and no catalyst to create the pearl of authentic awakening. This is precisely why the 10th-century Buddhist master Atisha famously chose the most annoying and irritating man he could find as his personal attendant.

Is it always shadow projection, though? Aren't some people just really annoying? How can we tell the difference between psychological projection and somebody simply being an asshole?

Sometimes being annoyed *is* a genuine response to someone doing something that is genuinely annoying or unjust. However, when our level of annoyance far outweighs the annoying action, or if we feel the need to keep ranting about how annoying that person was, then almost certainly a shadow projection has been triggered within us.

An inflated emotional response is almost always indicative of projection, so be aware of any situation in which your emotional response is out of proportion to the action committed or the words said.

Transpersonal psychology pioneer Ken Wilber has a model for recognizing shadow projection. He says, 'If a person or thing in the environment *informs us*, we probably aren't projecting. On the other hand, if it *affects us*, then we probably are.'[8]

Let's say I see someone drop litter. If my peace of mind remains pretty unaffected, even though I may discern that their action is unwise and even decide to act upon what I have observed (such as dispose of the litter myself or challenge them on their actions), there is probably no shadow projection. If, however, I experience an inflated emotional response *disproportionate to the act* (such as yelling, whether internally or externally, 'People like that shouldn't be allowed to walk the streets!'), then I can be sure that there is shadow projection going on around the act of dropping litter.

'It can't be shadow projection, I've never littered in my life!' you may protest. In that case, try to focus less on the act itself and more on the *energy* of the act. This is vital when looking at shadow projection: focus on the *energy, not the act*.

In the case of littering, the energy of the act might be one of selfishness and lack of regard and respect. You may have never littered in your life, but can you really say that you've never acted selfishly or with a lack or regard or respect?

Reminded of Who We Used to Be

Another type of shadow projection, and one of the most triggering for many people, is seen when we react to unacceptable traits that we used to display but believe that we don't display anymore.

For example, we are more likely to be triggered by the self-righteous arrogance of another person if we used to act arrogantly ourselves, or by the infuriating cyclists who run red lights when we used to run red lights too but have recently decided not to do so (I'm still working on that one).

This form of projection can work with more virtuous traits too. The 'happy-go-lucky' positivity of another person might trigger and irritate us if we used to be like this ourselves, but are no longer that way as a result of depression or distressing life experiences, for example. This is a particularly fascinating aspect of projection, but also particularly tricky to spot.

Secretly Wishing to Be That Way

Finally, there is the projection of seeing a trait in another person that we secretly want to display, but daren't. This one has caught me waist-deep in shadow projection more times than I care to remember.

One of my main annoyances in life used to be self-appointed gurus who said whatever they liked and then proclaimed its 'ultimate truth' because it was 'channelled from a higher power' (one that only they had contact with) and thus 'beyond dispute'. This kind of behaviour used to really trigger me. After exploring other explanations, I had to consider the uncomfortable possibility that perhaps there was part of me that wished I could do the same.

Was there really a part of me that secretly wished I could just teach or write what I liked rather than go through the often rigorous academic study and spiritual training that are required in Tibetan Buddhism? Although it makes me cringe to admit it, it was definitely true. In fact, I could see multiple times when I'd done similar things to those 'gurus' myself, but been too ashamed to admit it.

Once I was aware of the shadow projection, I could at least crack a little smile when I felt myself being triggered, and slowly, over time, begin to let it go. I still get triggered by this sometimes, but at least now I am triggered from a place of greater awareness and humour than before. It's a long road, though.

Once we are conscious of our shadow projections, we can be kinder, more loving human beings, because we not only see how we are projecting onto others, but also how they are projecting too, and with that we don't have to take everything so personally anymore.

We can even learn to become amused and fascinated when we catch ourselves projecting. A feeling of 'Oh wow, this guy is really triggering my shadow!' can provide humour that acts as a buffer zone, allowing us to respond consciously rather than react unconsciously.

So, the next time something or someone really annoys you, before reacting, try to take a moment to ask yourself, 'Am I ever like that?', 'Was I ever like that in the past?' and 'Do I secretly wish I could be like that sometimes?' Very often the answer will be affirmative to all three, and with that you will gain insight into your shadow and might even feel a bit less annoyed too.

Projection Reveals the Golden Shadow: The Acorn and the Oak Tree

Our golden shadow is also projected onto others. It appears not as irritation, but as admiration and awe.

Imagine an acorn, surrounded by fallen leaves, looking up in wonder at the oak tree from which it fell, thinking, *Wow! It's so tall! So magnificent! There's no way I could ever be like that. It's crazy to think that I could ever be an oak tree.*

And yet, with the right conditions (moisture, light and nutrients), the acorn will transform into an oak tree whether it believes it can or not.

In the same way, whether we believe in our highest potential or not, with the right conditions (the moisture of acceptance, the light of awareness and the nutrients of integration), the oak tree of our true nature will manifest naturally.

The traits we admire in others are often our own disowned or unrecognized potential. So, any strong feeling of awe or admiration for someone is indicative of the projection of our own golden shadow.

Just as we may fear the dark shadow, so we may be in awe of the golden, as the talents, potential and unseen capacity within us are projected onto those whose capacities we admire. But, as Professor of Psychology Geoffrey Lantz told me, 'If you recognize and resonate with the greatness in someone else, then you inherently have that greatness within yourself, otherwise you wouldn't be able to recognize it in the first place!'[9]

Anytime you find yourself gushing with praise for someone, take a moment to ask yourself, 'Am I ever like that?' and 'Do I have the potential to be like that?'

Science backs up this theory too. A study published in the *Journal of Personality and Social Psychology* found that a person's tendency to describe others in positive terms was an important indicator of the positivity of their own personality traits.[10] The researchers discovered particularly strong associations between how positively a person judged others and how enthusiastic, happy, kind-hearted and capable they described themselves as and were described as by others.

Golden shadow projection displays itself in multifarious ways, but the three main forms are:

- *traits that we deny we have but aspire to:* 'I can't dance very well, but I've always wanted to and wish that I could.'

- *traits that are unseen yet currently activated in us, which makes us resonate with them in another person:* 'Yes, I totally get what you're saying. I feel like that too! You're really inspiring me to dance.'

- *traits that we used to have and secretly wish we still had:* 'I used to be a great dancer, just like you. You are really brilliant; I wish I could dance like you.'

So, anytime you feel your heart open with admiration, resonance or joyful congratulation, you can be sure that the *energy* of what you are admiring, resonating with or congratulating will also be found in some form within you.

Exercise: Recognizing the Projected Shadow

How can we reclaim those parts of ourselves that we have been so busy projecting onto other people? How can we accept and express the talents and brilliance that we hide?

The first step is to recognize those traits. This exercise (inspired by a similar one in David Richo's *Shadow Dance*) will help you do exactly that. We will be making lists, so you might like to get a pen or pencil.

Step 1

- Take a moment to come into an awareness of your breath. Just notice when you are breathing in and notice when you are breathing out.

- Notice with awareness three inhalations and exhalations before you begin.

- Without thinking about it too much, and definitely without censoring yourself, list three traits that you *strongly dislike* or find *unfavourable* about members of the following groups:

  - *the same sex*

  - *the same profession*

  - *the same nationality*

Step 2

- Now, list three traits you *really admire* about members of the following groups:

  - *the same sex*

  - *the same profession*

  - *the same nationality*

Step 3

- Read through both the dislike and admire lists and take a moment to consider the following questions:

    - *'How do I feel when I look at the lists?'*

    - *'Do I ever embody or have I ever embodied any of these traits?'*

    - *'Do I ever wish that I could embody any of these traits?'*

    - *'Do any of these traits appear in my dreams?'*

Step 4

- If you like, you can add some of the things that you disliked about the three groups to your 'Aspects of My Dark Shadow' list and some of the things that you admired to your 'Aspects of My Golden Shadow' list (*see pages 24–27*). Not every trait you listed will be part of your shadow, but a few definitely will be.

Step 5

- Take a moment to dedicate the beneficial energy of this exercise to yourself and to all living beings.

We are still in the 'Meeting the Shadow' stage of our work, so for now we need do nothing more than bear witness to our shadow projections with loving acceptance for integration to gradually start to occur.

This forms the basis of what the Indian philosopher Krishnamurti famously referred to as 'the seeing is the doing'.

The Seeing Is the Doing

Much of our harmful behaviour can be traced to unseen shadow material: I don't see my anger, so I project it onto others, or I don't see my divine potential, so I have low self-esteem. This shadow material can be integrated through any practice that helps us to see what was previously unseen in our mind.

By seeing, recognizing and witnessing our shadow content, we not only gain freedom from the potentially harmful effects of projecting that unseen energy, but we also harness that energy to fuel the fire of our awakening. This is a four-step process:

1. Seeing

2. Recognizing (naming)

3. Witnessing

4. Integrating

Seeing

The first step asks that we see what is there. This requires opening our eyes and switching on the light of awareness. The exercises in this book will help us to do that, for example, 'I see that I am scared of rejection.'

Recognizing

Seeing is not enough, though. We have to *recognize* what we are seeing. We might recognize that it is a shadow trait or golden potential.

For example: 'I *recognize* that this fear is a recurring shadow trait that appears in various areas of my life.'

We are empowered through recognition, because we now know more than we did before.

If we like, we can then give what we have recognized a name: 'fear of rejection' or 'golden artist', for example. Through naming the shadow aspect, we remove its mask and see through its mystery.* Naming is an act of power: once named, the shadow trait will often start to surrender its energy.

---

* This is a theme often found in myths and fairy tales: saying the true name of an adversary will often subdue their power.

Witnessing

Next comes the witnessing stage. This is quite subtle, because essentially we do nothing, but it is a very *intentional* act of doing nothing. To make changes in our physical world, we usually have to take some action, but in our mental world, simply bearing impartial witness is, in fact, a very powerful act.

At the witnessing stage, it is essential that we don't try to fix or change what we have recognized or named, just bear witness to it with compassionate acceptance.

Integrating

The fourth stage happens spontaneously, maybe straight after we have witnessed the recognized shadow aspect or sometimes gradually over the days or weeks that follow.

***

Every exercise in this book is designed to get you to the first and second stages: seeing and recognizing/naming. The witnessing stage is down to you. If you can resist the habitual urge to correct or get rid of your shadow aspects and just witness them with compassionate acceptance, then the integrating stage will most definitely occur. It might take weeks to move from recognition to being able to witness what you have recognized with compassionate acceptance, so be gentle with yourself and don't rush the process.

Golden Shadow Heroes

Now let's learn how to see, recognize and witness some of our golden shadow traits. The heroes and heroines we choose to revere are almost always indicative of golden shadow projection, as we refuse to bear witness to our noble traits while seeing them reflected in others.

Archetypal characters such as the villain, the wise old woman and the fool are present in the majority of myths, stories and Hollywood films, but it's often the heroes or heroines we connect with most. By pinpointing those we particularly admire, we gain strong indications of where our golden shadow lies.

Of course, when considering this we must focus on the energy, not the act. For example, if you feel a strong resonance with the character Katniss Everdeen from *The Hunger Games* books and films, it doesn't necessarily mean that you should take up archery and start a rebellion against the Capitol. But it may indicate that untapped vulnerability, emotional strength and courageous beliefs are part of your golden shadow. If you feel a strong emotional connection with the character of James Bond, it doesn't necessarily mean that you have the potential to be an MI6 agent with a licence to kill, but it may indicate golden shadow elements of bravery, individuality and the questioning of authority for the greater good.

Who are your heroes and heroines?

Exercise: Golden Shadow Heroes

Let's see what your favourite heroes or heroines reveal about the contents of your golden shadow.

Step 1
- Take a moment to come into an awareness of your breath. Just notice when you are breathing in and notice when you are breathing out.

- Notice with awareness three inhalations and exhalations before you begin.

- Choose one of your favourite heroes, heroines or central protagonists from a film, book, story or play.

- List three of their admirable characteristics, for example kindness, audacity and courage.

Step 2

- Go through the same process with either two more of your favourite heroes or heroines and perhaps even with one of your favourite celebrities too.

Step 3

- Look at your list of admirable characteristics and ask yourself:

    - *'Do I ever wish I embodied any of these traits?'*

    - *'Do I ever embody or have I ever embodied any of these traits myself?'*

    - *'Do any of these traits appear in my dreams?'*

Step 4

- If you like, you can add some of these admirable characteristics to your 'Aspects of My Golden Shadow' list (*see page 24*).

Step 5

- Take a moment to dedicate the beneficial energy of this exercise to yourself and to all living beings.

When I first did this exercise, I chose the character Tommy, played by Tom Hardy, in the martial arts film *Warrior*. His vulnerability, authenticity and refusal to give up didn't just resonate with me, they *affected* me. And so I knew that there must be golden shadow projection at play.

After watching the film again, I realized why I'd been so affected by it. It isn't just about martial arts, it's about healing fraternal relationships, and so at the end of the film I wrote my brother the email that I should have written him years before and apologized to him for things from our childhood about which I was still ashamed. That email changed things between us, and now we do martial arts together, just as the brothers do in the film, and are closer than ever before.

In Your Dreams...

The integration of unconscious shadow material happens in large part in our sleep, so remembering dreams and writing them down enhances the process. It is possible to do this work and not keep a dream diary, but to really know the shadow, keeping a dream diary is a must. By writing down our dreams we start to see our shadow displayed on the page before us.

Writing down our dreams pays homage to them and, more importantly, reinforces the habit of viewing them as something valuable. Once we see dreams as valuable, we will naturally start to recall them with more ease and our dreaming mind may even respond by giving us dreams of more psychological value.

Once we start to remember, document and relate to our dreams, we not only start making friends with our shadow, but we prepare the ground for becoming lucid within our dreams. It comes down to this: 'The more conscious you are of your dreams, the easier it will be to become conscious *within* your dreams.'[11]

Exercise: Five Steps to Keeping a Dream Diary

1. Whenever you wake up from a dream, recall as much of it as you can and then write it down or document it in some way. Many people like to type their dream recollections onto a tablet or a smartphone, while others like to use a notebook and pen. Either method is fine.

2. You don't need to record every detail – you'll know what feels worth noting and what doesn't. Focus on the main themes and feelings, the general narrative and any strange anomalies or notable emotional content that you can recall.

3. If you wake up in the middle of the night after a vivid dream, try to make a few notes there and then, because you might have forgotten the dream by the morning.

4. Try to write something in your dream diary every morning if you can, even if it's just: 'I know that I've been dreaming, but I can't remember what about.'

5. You don't need to spend ages documenting your dreams; in fact, you'll be surprised how much you can write up in just five minutes. I rarely spend more than five minutes writing down my dreams at night, but I often expand them further over breakfast.

If you're new to dream work, don't be disappointed if you only remember a few snippets of each dream. That's fine for now. Work from where you are and gradually you'll start recalling more and more.

In Part II we'll learn how to decode the shadow content in our dreams and explore lucid dreaming, but for now I would simply ask you to start writing down your dreams and being aware of any shadow themes that might be appearing.

CHAPTER 4

CHILDHOOD SHADOW

*'Every child is an artist. The problem is how to
remain an artist once they grow up.'*

Pablo Picasso[1]

Exploring the childhood shadow can be delicate work, so before
we start, we should explore the three pillars of shadow work.

The Three Pillars of Shadow Work

Let's start by looking at acceptance, the most crucial of all the
pillars.

Acceptance

Shadow work is fundamentally about showing love to that which
we are yet to love. Acceptance and love are closely linked,
because to fully accept yourself is to extend your love to every
part of yourself, however shadowy some of them may seem.

Paradoxically, once we can accept that we have certain
shadow traits within us and are brave enough to tell them,
'Okay, I see you and I accept that you are part of me,' they
actually start to diminish.

The use of the word 'acceptance' here doesn't mean the
approval or endorsement of harmful mind-states or situations,

though. Imagine we have broken our toe. We don't have to approve of having broken our toe, but we do have to accept that it is broken before we can start healing it.

So, acceptance is a prerequisite to healing – and to shadow integration. Why? Because the conditions for integration are created by and dependent upon acceptance. Non-acceptance only creates internal struggle and psychological conflict.

Psychologist Robert Holden says, 'It's the emotions that we judge the most, that we are the most ashamed of and most afraid of, that we must meet with the most acceptance. With acceptance, something starts to change in the shadow. It starts to transform.'[2]

I asked Robert what he thought happened when we didn't accept our shadow traits.

He replied, 'If we are not currently accepting our shadow traits, then we are probably suppressing, rejecting, repressing, defending and attacking them, and ultimately accusing everyone else of having them more than us! Acceptance is vital.'

Friendliness

Once we accept things, we can start to become friendly towards them. Shadow work asks us to look at things that we usually shy away from or reject, but, as the brilliant Tibetan master Mingyur Rinpoche says, 'If you reject an emotion, it will become your enemy. If you indulge it, it becomes the boss of you. So what do we do with our emotions? What's the best method? Face them and make friends with them!'[3]

So, cultivating an attitude of friendliness towards ourselves and others lies at the core of shadow integration. Unconditional friendliness towards our weakness and our strengths, towards our dark and our light, and, crucially, towards those who, however painfully, expose our shadows is vital to the process.

Whether dark or golden, our shadow is simply the unintegrated parts of ourselves, so to make friends with it is to make friends with ourselves.

Kindness

Everywhere we are unkind to ourselves, everywhere we reject ourselves, everywhere we have abandoned ourselves, we find the shadow. It was unkindness that created it and so it is kindness that integrates it.

Kindness to the shadow goes beyond friendliness and moves us into the process of proactively seeking out ways to show kindness to it. This will make us kinder to others too, not only because we are preventing more shadow content from being created in ourselves, but also because we are more likely to show kindness to the shadows of those we meet.

Be kind to yourself throughout this shadow work process too. Being kind enough to recognize 'I'm not quite ready to look at that yet' is just as important as being kind enough to recognize 'I've let this thing rule me for too long. I am ready to integrate that shadow.'

Exercise: Hand on Heart Meditation

If at any point during your shadow work you feel overwhelmed or upset and want to come back into mindful alignment, or simply need to show some kindness to yourself, I recommend doing this wonderful little self-compassion practice which I learned through Mindfulness Association UK.

Let's learn it now, so that we have it down for when we might need it.

Step 1
- Place your right hand over your heart. Feel the connection between your hand and your chest.

Step 2

- Say to yourself, either internally or out loud:

    *This is a moment of difficulty. Everybody has moments of difficulty.
    I am going to be kind to myself in this moment of difficulty.*

- Alternatively, you could say:

    *I am feeling pain. I acknowledge that I'm suffering.
    I show myself love. I show myself kindness.*

Step 3

- Take a moment to breathe out deeply, relaxing into the out-breath with an 'ah' sound.

- Simply rest in the relaxation of the out-breath.

The Science of Kindness

Kindness can actually improve our physical health too.

A review of 50 scientific studies exploring the effects of kindness, altruism and benevolence by researchers at Case Western Reserve University School of Medicine, in Cleveland, Ohio, USA, found, unsurprisingly, that generosity and compassion had a positive effect on people's health and well-being.

Research showed a 44 per cent reduction in early death among people who regularly volunteered for a charity, which was a greater benefit to their health than exercising four times a week.[4]

The researchers concluded: 'These studies indicate that we're dealing with something that's extremely powerful. Ultimately, the process of cultivating a positive emotional state through pro-social behaviours and kindness may lengthen your life.'[5]

The Inventory of Love

With the three pillars of acceptance, friendliness and kindness in mind, let's go back to childhood, which is where we start creating our shadow.

I acknowledge that many people have experienced some form of childhood abuse on some level, be it mental, emotional or physical. However, it is not within the scope of this book (nor my expertise) to safely explore and incorporate the painful shadow effects of childhood abuse. Instead, this book focuses on working through the more general shadows that are most commonly experienced in childhood.

His Holiness the Dalai Lama has said, 'Every child is fresh and their basic nature is one of compassion,'[6] but as children we learn from those around us and soon lose touch with that compassionate freshness. We take note of what brings acceptance and love from others and what brings rejection and lack of love. We learn to equate being good with being loved. We take a careful inventory of which parts of ourselves we should present to others and which parts we should hide from them.

This process is inherently culturally specific – for example, the child of progressive parents who value free expression will have a very different inventory from a child of strict, conservative parents.

Some of the first shadow content for Western children is often around nakedness, as we realize that being naked in public is frowned upon. Running around our home naked might be fine, but on the day that we try to leave the house naked we receive a rebuttal of loud words which, though we cannot understand them, we decode as 'My naked body is bad'. So we disown our nakedness and force it into the shadowy 'cellar of the unacceptable'.

Body shame may soon be joined by anger or rowdiness, both of which we're taught are unbefitting for 'good' little boys and girls to display.

Burying Our Treasure

In many ways, this process plays an important role in our development, but the problem is that we struggle to separate the different aspects of our emotional energies, and so if we are forced to bury our rowdiness as children then in our adult life we may find ourselves without the vitality that is sourced from the same energy system. If we buried our anger in childhood, we may inadvertently have buried some of our assertiveness too, and if our sexuality has been rejected, part of our creativity may have gone with it.

The same process occurs with our golden shadow, and so begins the burial of our childhood exuberance. Being a great singer or having lots of charisma may have been seen as a threat to our social compatibility and thus been unacceptable to us when we were children, so we may have pushed these traits into the back of our mind, where they coalesced into the golden shadow.

If we are to 'fit in', which in late childhood becomes a seemingly vital necessity for most of us, then our flowering brilliance must be tempered and hidden away in the shadows just as much as our fear and shame. It seems that the brightness of our being threatens our sapling sense of self just as much as our darkness does.

From a psychological perspective, the formation of our sense of self is created in response to the culture around us, which requires us to trim off the top shoots of our highest potential if we are to sit neatly within the hedgerows of social normality.

So, is all lost? Are we forever stuck in the rut that we created in childhood or the hole that we have dug for ourselves more recently? Definitely not. The shadow wants to be known and its energy wants to be released. Integrating the shadow isn't concerned with who we *were*, but who we *may become*.

No Questions Asked

David Richo believes that children do not instinctively defend themselves against their mother and that because their discriminating ego is not yet formed, the shadow messages from their parents or primary care-givers are planted straight into their unconscious without question.

Essentially, in a child's mind, the 'stranger danger' concept is not seen to be applicable to its parents and primary care-givers. This means that the personal *opinions* of these people are not taken as mere opinions, but are installed in the unconscious as uncensored *facts*. When they offer a critical or unhelpful opinion about us – 'You can't dance' or 'You're not clever' – we don't question or evaluate it, but install it directly into our psychological operating system. Then we use it as the benchmark for what should be relegated to our shadow side.

When I first encountered this idea, I was shocked. It suggests that every time a young child hears an opinion from a parent, care-giver or authority figure, they may well accept it as truth and allow it to shape their emerging sense of self.

Inevitably, our parents add to our shadow even more when they project their own unintegrated shadow onto us. Their limiting beliefs ('Being an artist isn't a job!') and cultural preferences ('Marriage is between a man and woman!') help to create our emerging shadow just as much as our own unique predilections and character traits.

Musing on this point, shadow expert Robert A. Johnson believes that integrating our own shadow is the greatest gift we can give our children, because in so doing we are offering them a clean psychological heritage.

In her book *Daring Greatly*, Brené Brown mentions a client who loved art as a child but once overheard his uncle say to his father, 'You're raising a faggot artist now?' as he pointed at his artwork taped to the refrigerator. The little boy never painted again, but his inner artist will still be there, waiting for him in the light of his golden shadow.

The Inner Critic

Painful early life experiences in which we encounter hurtful attitudes toward us also create an 'inner critic' or 'critical inner voice', which often manifests as a 'negative internal commentary on who we are and how we behave'.[7] This is not our true voice, it is the echo of a dozen well-meaning but mistaken care-givers who have unwittingly installed a program of criticism in our mind.

Dr Eric Berne, the author of *Games People Play*, refers to this inner voice as '25,000 hours of parental recordings' playing inside our head. The broken record of 'You're too fat for that', 'You're stupid' or 'They don't like you' has often been going round for so long that we accept it as the elevator music of the mind. But when we fail to identify and separate our truth from the outdated opinion of the inner critic, we allow it to impact our behaviour and shape the direction of our life.

New research from clinical psychology believes that 'by identifying, separating from and acting against this destructive thought process, you will grow stronger, while your inner critic grows weaker'.[8] So the next time you identify the inner critic, try saying its opinions out loud. It seems paradoxical, but research has shown that 'the process of formulating and verbalizing negative thoughts lessens the destructive effect of the inner voice'[9] and helps to release the stagnant emotional blocks they create.

By doing this, you will also see that they are often far too generalized ('You don't know what you're talking about' or 'Nobody likes you') to be true all the time and so you cannot call them 'your truth'. Instead, you can offer a new opinion, a truer one, which may help change the music of the past and set the record straight.

Forgiveness

> 'Forgiveness is the fragrance that a violet
> sheds on the heel that crushes it.'
> **Anon**

Although the opinions of our primary care-givers help us to create our shadow, what good would blaming them do? We know that blame just creates more shadow.

Who we are is not our fault, but it is our responsibility. Fortunately, our *ability to respond* to our current shadow is not predicated on the actions of the past, but on our willingness to forgive in the present.

As we cast our mind back to childhood and remember the things that were said to us, the wounds that were inflicted on us and the limiting critical programs that were installed in our mind, we may inevitably come across grievances and bitterness. The antidote is forgiveness, but what is forgiveness and how does it relate to the shadow?

Robert Holden, who specializes in this field, explained, 'Whatever you haven't forgiven is your shadow. The shadow is made up of whatever you are unwilling to show love to, and what you don't forgive, you don't love. The process of forgiveness is to bring love to what you have not forgiven. It arises from the willingness to bring love to a situation.'[10]

Brooding over past grievances can be like picking a scab: if we do this, it will never heal. For many of us, our heart is a patchwork of scars from the wounds that we suffered at the hands of others – and so often from ourselves too. Forgiveness allows these wounds to heal. We will still carry the scars, but the wounds will start to heal.

Freeing Up Hard-drive Space

I've found that holding onto grievances takes up a lot of hard-drive space in my mind. All of the individual apps of resentment and bitterness keep running in the background, making my mental laptop run at half-speed.

But I've also found that forgiveness frees up this hard drive, uninstalls the resentment apps and makes me feel lighter and more liberated from the weight of the past.

When I shared this image with Robert, he said, 'Exactly! Forgiveness sets us free. We don't forgive to be spiritual or good, we do it to be free. To forgive is to decide that "From this moment forward I will not be limited by that grievance. I will still feel it, but I will not be limited by it." There has to be a moment when we think, *Is holding onto this grievance helping me anymore or just weighing me down?*'[11]

And yet many of us actually don't want to forgive. Why is this?

'Who Am I without My Wounds?'

Our ego identity is sometimes threatened when we forgive. It may ask, 'Who am I without my grievances? Who am I without my resentment?' These questions challenge who we think we are and so make us feel uncomfortable.

Robert believes, 'We have resistance to forgiveness and even fear of it – a fear founded on the misperception that if we forgive, we are condoning the unforgivable action and letting the other person get away with it. If we feel this resistance, then it is important to meet the part of us that doesn't want to forgive and to ask ourselves: "If I were to forgive this person, which part of me would be disappointed?"'[12]

I've often struggled with forgiveness. I'd convince myself that I'd forgiven someone but whenever their name was mentioned, a kind of mental footnote would appear, reminding me of the past grievance, complete with the date when it occurred and a brief synopsis of the unforgivable deed. And with that I would cringingly have to admit to myself that I hadn't fully forgiven them. Part of me had, but not the whole of me.

Robert has an exercise in the book *Life Loves You*, co-authored with Louise Hay, in which he asks you to select a person you have a grievance towards. It could be anyone, even yourself if you like. Whoever it is, ask yourself, 'From 0 to 100 per cent, how much have I forgiven this person?'

Once you have decided upon your percentage, 75 per cent for example, you then ask yourself, 'Am I willing to forgive this person 80 per cent? How would that feel?' and then once you have found a place on the 'Forgiveness Scale' that you feel comfortable with, you affirm, 'I am willing to forgive this person 82 per cent,' and with that the healing begins, because it is simply our *willingness* to forgive that orchestrates the healing.

Even if only 1 per cent of us is willing to forgive, that can be enough to begin with. The healing that forgiveness brings will begin to seep in slowly, drop by drop, and eventually bring us back to a place of love.

The Science of Forgiveness

Forgiveness is good for your health. Dr David Hamilton pointed me to a study published in the International Journal of Psychophysiology that showed that forgiveness had the potential to lower blood pressure and the levels of stress hormones throughout the cardiovascular system.[13]

It also benefits our mental health. The Stanford University HOPE projects gave forgiveness training to several men and women who had tragically lost family members in the conflict in Northern Ireland. After the forgiveness training, most of them registered significant reductions in hurt, anger, stress and depression.[14]

The overall benefits of forgiveness are so great that Dr Frederic Luskin of the Stanford Medical Centre says, 'Forgiveness has both psychosocial and physiological value ... and may be, as the religious traditions have been claiming all along, the rich path to greater peace.'[15]

The Bag That We Drag Behind Us

The poet Robert Bly calls the shadow 'the bag that we drag behind us'. He describes it a huge sack full of our fear, shame and secrets, which we drag through life and which weighs us down.

He believes that we create this invisible bag as children. As a way of keeping our parents' love, we place all the parts of ourselves that they don't like into the bag. But we shove in much more besides. Some children are forced to put the loud *enthousiasmós* of childhood in the bag, and with it goes their joy. Others, as we saw earlier, are told to put their anger in the bag, and with it goes their assertiveness and decisive clarity. Some grow up being taught that sex is shameful and so they put their sexual energy in the bag, along with much of their vitality and creativity.

Every time we consign something to our bag, we lose energy. The psychological energy, the *chi*, that lies in anger, fear, sexuality and desire is lost when we stuff them into our bag. The contents of our bag weigh us down, constrict us, limit our expression and restrict access to the power within it.

By the time we go to school our bag is already quite large, and then, as authority is transferred to our teachers and to children of a higher status, their opinions dictate what we stuff in there.

By adulthood, we have become so accustomed to stuffing anything we don't want to show to others into our bag that we continue doing it simply out of habit. I suggest that we break this habit.

Once we explore the contents of our bag, we can begin the alchemical process of transforming this heavy emotional baggage into beneficial change and regaining our energy, our *chi*, our psychological power, and expressing ourselves fully, just as we did as children.

In his seminal book *The Things They Carried*, Vietnam veteran Tim O'Brien described the heavy weight that the soldiers carried in their bags. He listed their physical contents – grenades, ammo, flares, rations and lucky amulets – and also their psychological contents – 'they carried ... their grief, terror, love, longing'[16] as well as their shameful memories, fear of death and hidden secrets.

We may not be in a warzone ourselves, but Buddhist nun Pema Chödrön says that we're all carrying round unnecessary baggage and the job of the spiritual warrior is to open their bag and looks closely at what it contains. By doing this, she says we will understand that a lot of it isn't needed anymore and can start to take responsibility for the direction of our life.

Exercise: What's in Your Bag?

We all carry things, so I ask you, 'What's in your bag?'

Step 1

- Find yourself a pen and a sheet of paper.

- Take a moment to come into an awareness of your breath. Just notice when you are breathing in and notice when you are breathing out.

- Notice with awareness three inhalations and exhalations before you begin.

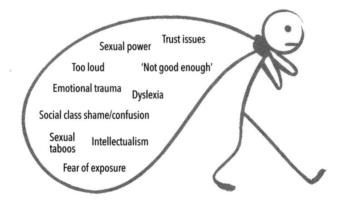

Figure 1: The bag that we drag

Step 2

- Using the diagram above as a guide, draw a stickman picture of yourself with the bag that you drag behind you. Be sure to leave some space above your bag, as we will be adding some extra bits later.

- Take some time to write or depict the contents of your bag: all the aspects of yourself that you don't yet love and that you hide from others – your shame, traumas, fears, unlived dreams, taboos and secrets. You might like to use your 'Aspects of My Dark Shadow' list for reference (*see page 24*).

What parts of yourself did you consign to your bag during childhood? If you can remember, write them in too.

Don't censor yourself – be honest and courageous. You don't have to share the contents of your bag with anyone. As with all these exercises, you can't get this wrong.

Step 3

- Take a moment to look through the contents of your bag and remind yourself that nothing there is 'bad', it is just unintegrated.

- Explore the following questions:

    - *How much of the bag's contents were you aware of already?*

    - *What do you feel when you look into your bag – shame, regret, authenticity, joy?*

    - *How would you feel if you were to reveal the contents of your bag to others?*

Step 4

- Now find a way to send loving acceptance to the contents of your bag.

    As you scan through its contents, you might like to recite an affirmation of loving acceptance such as:

    I see you. I show you my love.

As always, 'the seeing is the doing', so simply by becoming conscious of the contents of your bag, you will start to lighten its load.

Step 5

Take a moment to dedicate the beneficial energy of this exercise to yourself and to all living beings.

Seeing ourselves clearly is initially uncomfortable and embarrassing for many of us, as we see things we'd prefer not to see – arrogance, fear, shame, unlived dreams – but, as Pema Chödrön reminds us, 'These are not sins, but temporary, workable habits of mind, and the more we get to know them, the more they lose their power.'[17]

Exercise: Helium Balloons

Step 1

- Using the same diagram, draw several helium balloons above your bag with their strings attached to it. Use the diagram below as a guide.

- In each helium balloon, write or signify whatever lifts you up, helps you in life or lightens your load. This could include people, pets, objects, activities, hobbies, spiritual practices or teachers.

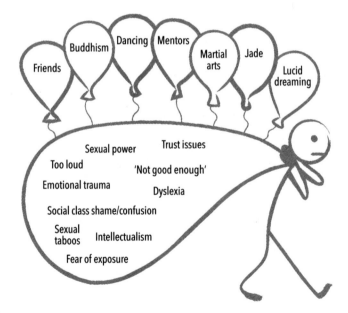

Figure 2: Lightening the load that we drag

Add in some of your beneficial character traits too. These can be anything from your habit of holding the door open for strangers to your enlightened potential.

Step 2

- Draw in another few balloons and write in them your golden shadow aspects. These might include some of the things from your 'Aspects of My Golden Shadow' list (*see page 24*), including your superpower and what you want to be when you grow up.

Include any untapped potentials that have not been fully manifested or that you tend to hide from others. Forget modesty for a minute and write some fun future possibilities too ('*New York Times* bestselling author' or 'professional artist'). Within every crazy potential there will often be a seed of truth. Have fun with it.

Add in some more balloons containing traits from the 'Golden Shadow Heroes' exercise if you like.

Step 3

- Take a moment to look at your helium balloons and explore the following questions:

  - *How many of the balloons were you aware of already?*

  - *What do you feel when you look at your balloons – gratitude, melancholy, joy, surprise?*

  - *How able are you to reveal the golden traits they contain to others?*

Step 4

- Now, find a way to send loving acceptance and gratitude to your helium balloons.

As you scan through them you might like to recite an affirmation of loving acceptance such as:

I see you, I show you my love.

Step 5

- Take a moment to witness both your bag and your helium balloons.
- Dedicate the beneficial energy of this exercise to yourself and to all living beings.

After doing these exercises at one of my workshops, a woman called Nikki, who works as a change management consultant, emailed me, saying:

> As they say, 'shit gets real' when you turn inwards and I've felt that something has shifted. I feel more present now and less shackled by my demons. I've struggled with addictive and impulsive behaviour since my teens, but through this work I've been feeling more positive about integrating this stuff. Actually, this is the first time I've really had a proper look at my shadow self and recognized it's not as scary as I'd thought.

Even after adding in all the helpful helium balloons, these exercises might still evoke quite powerful emotions. If you feel the need for a moment of self-compassion, please take some time to do the Hand on Heart Meditation (see page 53).

In Your Dreams...

The hypnagogic state is the transitional state of mind between wakefulness and sleep. It's the drowsy, in-between stage often characterized by hypnagogic imagery – the dreamy visual or sometimes conceptual displays that flash and fade before our mind's eye as we drift off to sleep.

The hypnagogic state is actually a type of very light sleep, but is experienced by many people as more of a heavy drowsiness than sleep, and it's often accompanied by alpha brainwave patterns of relaxed wakefulness. It's these brainwaves and the deep relaxation they produce that make this such a powerful state of mind. As is indicated by the word 'hypnagogic', it is not dissimilar to the hypnotic trance state, and so can be used to plant hypnotic suggestions.

Exercise: Hypnagogic Golden Shadow

Why not harness the power of the hypnagogic state to plant some golden shadow affirmations as you fall asleep tonight? This will not only help to manifest those golden potentials in your waking life, but will have a powerful effect on your dream life too.

The Buddhist dream teachings say that the last thought before you fall asleep can flavour the whole night's sleep, so if your last thought is of your inner gold then you could be in for a very interesting night.

Step 1

- Choose three of the untapped golden shadow traits that you aspire to manifest fully into your life. Use your 'Aspects of My Golden Shadow' list for inspiration if you like (*see page 24*).

Step 2

- Lie down in bed and close your eyes. The aim of this practice is to stay in the hypnagogic state mindfully, without entering the sleep that lies beyond it.

- As you drift into the hypnagogic state, recite the following statement in your mind:

  I befriend my golden shadow. I am the power of [insert each of the golden shadow traits one by one].

  For example, 'I befriend my golden shadow. I am the power of *authenticity*.' 'I befriend my golden shadow. I am the power of *intelligence*.' 'I befriend my golden shadow. I am the power of *divine grace*.'

Step 3

- After a few minutes of repeating the recitations, allow yourself to fall asleep, saturated with the beneficial energy of these affirmations.

Don't worry if you don't nail this technique straight away. For most of us, the hypnagogic state is habitually associated with falling into unconscious sleep, so it can take a few attempts to float into it without blacking out.

As with all the exercises in this book, take your time with this. And don't worry if some of the exercises don't resonate with you as much as others. Feel free to come back to your favourites as often as you like.

Meeting Our Shadow

And finally, to end our 'Meeting the Shadow' section of the book, let's imagine actually meeting our shadow in personified form.

We are going to invite our shadow sides, both dark and golden, to come and sit with us. We are going to imagine that they manifest before us and that we welcome them, take them by the hand and sit with them.

We will do this through a visualization exercise. Don't worry about whether you can visualize clearly; just relax into the immersive feeling of imagination. As the great meditation masters say, 'Imagination makes anything possible.'

Exercise: Meeting Our Shadow

I recommend doing this exercise using the guided meditation set to music that can be found at www.charliemorley.com/shadowexercises under the title 'Meeting Our Shadow', but if you would like to follow it without guidance then I have included the script below.

Step 1
- Just sitting, with your eyes open or closed (either is fine), breathing through your nose or mouth (either is fine), breathe deeply. Show your body that you love it enough to give it what it needs: breath.

You are totally safe. You are held lovingly by the beneficial motivation of this meditation. Relax deeply – deeply enough to look into your shadow.

Step 2

- Take a moment to think about the unloved parts of yourself that you find unacceptable to show to others.

- Think about the parts of your mind that you struggle to love: your anger, your fear, your past traumas, aspects of your sexuality that you fear may be frowned upon, perhaps.

- Take a moment to consider and to encounter the dark shadow parts of yourself.

- If shame, guilt or discomfort come up, don't turn away from them as you have done before, turn towards them.

Step 3

- Can you locate these dark shadow aspects in your body?

- Imagine that your dark shadow flows out of your body and manifests in physical form next to you. Your dark shadow is sitting next to you.

  It will only show you what you are ready for, so feel its energy fearlessly and greet it like an old friend.

Step 4

- Take your shadow by the hand and sit with it. Friendship starts with a smile, so smile at your shame, your fear, your guilt, or whatever form the energy takes.

  Encounter this energy with love. Hold its hand. Nothing more is needed. Feel it responding to your love.

Step 5

- And now take a moment to think about all the magnificent parts of yourself that you find unacceptable to show to others.

- Is there a part of yourself that you find too bright to show to others? Your true potential, your intuition, your divine light?

- Take a moment to encounter these golden shadow parts of yourself.

- If power, joy or strong energy come up, don't turn away from them as you have done before, turn towards them, greet them like old friends. They are part of you.

Step 6

- Can you locate these golden shadow aspects in your body?

- Imagine that your golden shadow flows out of your body and manifests in physical form next to you. Your golden shadow is sitting next to you.

  It will only show you what you are ready for, so feel its energy fearlessly and take it by the hand.

  Friendship starts with a smile, so smile at your divine light, your power, your golden potential…

  Encounter this energy with love. Hold its hand. Nothing more is needed. Feel it responding to your love.

Step 7

- And now, sitting between the dark and light shadows, repeat after me, in your own mind, in your own way, the following words:

  I am ready to love my shadow. I am ready to
  befriend both the dark and the bright.

Step 8

- Allow the imagined visualization to dissolve so that you are now sitting alone again.

Step 9

- With the knowledge that you have just connected lovingly with both aspects of your shadow, take a moment to dedicate the beneficial energy of the meteration to all yourself and all beings.

PART II

BEFRIENDING THE SHADOW

*'There are no strangers here; only
friends you haven't yet met.'*
W.B. YEATS[1]

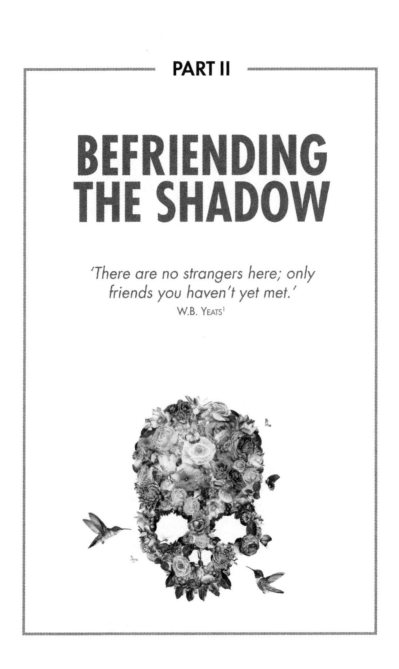

Now that we've met our shadow, both the dark and golden aspects, we're ready to befriend it.

As with all friendships, it'll take time and effort, but the effort will be worth its weight in gold as we reap the deep psycho-spiritual benefits of making an ally of our shadow side.

Some of the techniques we'll be exploring from now on might seem quite far out; they involve masks and mirrors, eye-gazing, imagined guardians around our bed and even calling forth our personified inner demons and lucidly embracing them in our dreams. Yes, really.

It's important that before we reach those exercises we ground our awareness solidly through a practice of often underestimated power: mindfulness meditation.

CHAPTER 5

MINDFULNESS MEDITATION

'Develop mindfulness. It is of great fruit and great benefit.'

Buddha[1]

Mindfulness meditation is highly recommended for all those wanting to explore the shadow. Not only because mindfulness naturally leads to insights into shadow content, but also because shadow work requires the strong and stable mind that mindfulness cultivates.

What Is Mindfulness?

Mindfulness is a quality of mind that is *aware of the present moment* and mindfulness meditation is the process of fostering and cultivating that awareness.

Mindfulness is not about stopping our thoughts or clearing our mind, it is simply about being aware of what is happening in our mind, without preference or judgement. Whatever happens is okay. We just 'watch the parade of thoughts and emotions as if we were standing on a viewing platform'.[2]

It's all about getting to know our mind, and the more we get to know our own mind, the more we get to know and empathize with the minds of others. This process leads to more kindness and friendliness – two vital components of shadow work in both our dreams and our waking life.

As long as we are aware of what is happening as it is happening, without preference or judgement, we are practising mindfulness. It's deceptively simple: bear witness to your internal environment.

Although many people find that sitting in silence is the easiest way to engage this instruction, we can actually practise mindfulness in every action that we perform, whether we are eating, walking, sitting or, as we will find out later, dreaming.

If we watch the mind openly enough and with enough friendly curiosity, it will start revealing itself freely.* If we pounce on its display and start judging it or, even worse, trying to fix it, then it will close back up again, but if we leave thoughts alone they will naturally begin to subside.

Mindfulness gives you time. It opens up a buffer zone between stimulus and response, meaning that we don't get swept away by reactivity and habitual patterns. We get that *crucial quarter-second* to observe, to simply bear witness to what arises. It is a moment of fascination: 'Wow! Look at my anger or anxiety or joy emerging!' It is a moment in which we have a choice: to witness mindfully or react unconsciously.

Lama Yeshe Rinpoche advises taking it one step further and actually inviting whatever we usually turn away from *into* our meditation. When I spoke to him about it, he said, 'When you have identified the mind-state that is bothering you, you should sit there, relax and actually invite this emotion into your meditation. Whether it is fear, anxiety, jealousy, whatever it is, invite it in and introduce yourself to it, make friends with it.'³

---

* When mindfulness is present, the mind naturally comes into focus and balance. This balance allows fragmented shadow energies to be integrated – something they will do spontaneously when these conditions are created.

The Science of Mindfulness

Researchers at Harvard, Yale and Massachusetts Institute of Technology in America have now found conclusive evidence that regular periods of mindfulness meditation can actually alter the physical structure of our brain.

Some subjects who practised mindfulness meditation for just 30 minutes a day as part of a Massachusetts General Hospital study were shown to have changed the physical structure of their brain within the two-month period of the trial. Scientists found increases in grey-matter density of the hippocampus (an area responsible for learning and memory) and decreased density in the amygdala (an area responsible for anxiety and stress responses).[4]

Even with all this scientific proof, though, some people are still averse to the whole 'sitting alone in silence' thing. In fact, during a psychological experiment at Virginia University, 42 subjects were offered the choice of either sitting in silence or giving themselves electric shocks. Sixty-seven per cent of male subjects (but interestingly just 25 per cent of female subjects) 'chose to shock themselves rather than sit in silence'.[5]

The Tibetan word for meditation is *gom*, which means 'to become familiar with', and so meditation is all about becoming familiar with the mind. We simply sit, becoming familiar with ourselves, witnessing our psychology and listening to the music of our mind.

Most radio-edited songs are about three minutes long, so let's start listening to the music of our mind for a similar length of time.

Exercise: The Three-Minute Breathing Space Practice

This is a wonderfully accessible mindfulness exercise practised in the MBCT (Mindfulness Based Cognitive Therapy) model called the 'Three-Minute Breathing Space Practice'.

One of the founders of the technique is a professor of psychology called Zindel Segal, who realized that change depended on his clients being able to apply their mindfulness techniques in real-life situations but that the majority of the practices they were learning were too lengthy to be applicable in everyday life. So he set out to create something that could be done in just three minutes.

Each step of the Three-Minute Breathing Space is roughly one minute in length and the practice goes from wide focus to narrow to wide again. It's a great practice and can be done anywhere at any time, multiple times a day.

Step 1
- Bring your attention to your experience of the present moment in a wide and open manner. Expand your awareness.

- Notice your body sitting on the chair or cushion beneath you, notice the feelings or sensations that are present.

- Become a non-preferential container for thoughts. Just witness them with a broad panoramic awareness.

- Simply notice what's happening as it's happening, but without any need to change it.

- Hang out in this state for about a minute.

Step 2
- Now bring your focus to your breath. Just notice the sensations of breathing in and breathing out.

  Feel your chest or belly expanding as you breathe in and notice the release of your chest or belly as you relax and breathe out. You have been breathing since you woke up this morning (and long before that too), but how many breaths have you been aware of today? For the next minute, simply be aware of your breath.

Step 3

- And finally, release your focus on your breath and expand your awareness to include the sensations in your body, the thoughts and emotions in your mind and the sensation of sitting. Rest here for about a minute.

I advise practising the three-minute breathing space at least once a day. You can do it in a toilet cubicle at work, on the train, before a meeting or whenever you feel the need to be more present, calm and centred.

If at any point during your journey into the shadow you feel a bit scattered and want to get grounded again, be sure to come back to this practice. It can also be done when you are feeling strong shadow emotions.

When you feel ready for a longer and more formal mindfulness practice, try the 20-minute 'Settling, Grounding, Resting with Support' practice in Appendix I (*see page 232*). Again, this can be done at least once a day and comes highly recommended as a way to calm, ground and stabilize the mind.

CHAPTER 6

THE MASKS THAT WE WEAR

'Tear off the mask. Your face is glorious.'

Rumi[1]

Not only do we project our shadow onto others, we also project how we want to be seen by others. This is how we create our persona: the mask that we wear.

The mask of our persona is indicative not only of the self-image that we present to others, but also of what we hide from them. And as long as we keep hiding behind the mask of who we think we *should* be, we will never be free.

Most of us put all our energy into avoiding admitting that we have any seemingly shameful shadow traits. We daren't enter into the vulnerability of the human condition. This leads to a constricted, shame-based sense of who we think we are, which in turn makes it impossible to progress on the spiritual path. To embrace the shadow is to drop the mask and reveal our true face to the world.

Dropping the Mask

I uploaded the photo and instantly felt the fear. I knew that was the whole point of the exercise, but it didn't stop me feeling it.

I'd just uploaded a photo of a mask. On the outside of the mask I'd written the traits I presented to the world, but on the inside I'd exposed my deepest and most shameful shadow traits – exposed them to over 10,000 people on Facebook, Instagram and Twitter. Would that be too much for the 'love and light brigade' to handle? Had I just thrown my career away? I was supposed to be a meditator, a teacher, a role model even, but now people knew the side that I hid from others: a scared boy with impostor syndrome and sexual shame who sometimes watched porn and sometimes liked to fight.

Seriously regretting what I had just done, I thought it best to remove the post. I reached for my iPhone to delete the photo, but then ping, ping, ping, 'likes' were suddenly coming in one after the other, and then comments: 'So real and raw', 'Beautifully authentic' and 'Awesome honesty, thanks for sharing!'

People actually liked it. In fact, they loved it. Within the hour I was being tagged in the posts of people who had been so inspired that they had made their own masks and were uploading them to their Facebook pages in solidarity.

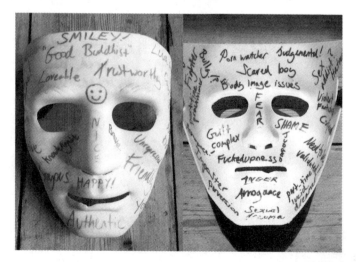

Figure 3: My mask from 2016

By the end of the day, that photo was my most liked, most shared and most commented-on social-media post ever. It turned out that on seeing me share my shadow side people felt empowered to start accepting theirs and move out of shame into the deep authenticity that lay behind the masks.

What I saw in my mask didn't shock me. I knew most of what I had been hiding – you know most of what you're hiding too – but what did shock me was how strong the aversion was when I considered sharing it with others. Still, I knew that strong aversion indicated strong suppressed energy and that if I could release and transmute that energy, I could find gold within.

Fascinatingly, I found that sharing the shameful habits written on the inside of my mask actually helped to release me from many of those habits. For example, the 'porn-watcher' bit is the shameful trait that often gets the most response at my workshops and leads to discussions about shame, masturbation and the internet generation. Interestingly, once I was able to admit publicly to this occasional but embarrassing habit, it actually had the effect of drastically reducing the occurrence of it. This is because shame perpetuates habit.

Habituated to Shame

Science has proved that shame perpetuates harmful habits and addiction because addiction is often based on a misplaced and unfulfilled need for bonding and connection.

An experiment first conducted at Simon Fraser University in Canada way back in the 1970s showed that when you offered water with morphine in it to isolated rats in empty cages, they all drank it and almost all overdosed and died from it. But when you offered it to rats in a cage that was full of other rats and nice food and things to do ('Rat Park', as the researchers called it), they almost never drank it and none of them got addicted to it.[2] Why? Because they had connection and bonding. When we are connected, we don't tend to get addicted to things or to create nearly as many destructive habits.

This theory was applied to humans in Portugal, with exactly the same effect: injecting drug use declined by 50 per cent because the money spent on shaming drug-users was instead spent on helping them bond and reconnect with society.[3]

Although the Rat Park experiment has been seen as an oversimplification by some, as someone who spent four years working as a drugs and alcohol outreach worker and who has struggled with addictive tendencies towards sex and drugs myself, I have seen first hand how shame perpetuates harmful habits.

When we shame ourselves, or are made to feel ashamed, we feel disconnected and are thus more likely to continue doing the shameful thing that makes us feel disconnected in the first place. But when we move into the vulnerability of witnessing our shameful habits and showing them love, our addiction to them wanes.

When considering shadow integration, the pioneer of Archetypal Psychology, James Hillman, thought of it as a problem of love and asked us to contemplate: 'How far can our love extend to the broken and ruined parts of ourselves, the disgusting and perverse?'[4]

We have a choice: to keep letting shame make us feel unworthy of love or to consciously witness, and perhaps even reveal, our shame with compassion. To really make progress, we have to do something that may seem quite paradoxical: we have to accept the parts of ourselves that we dare not show and learn to love our Magnificent Messiness.

The philosopher Tim Freke once told me how in the Eleusinian Mysteries of ancient Greece you would be expected to make a confession to the community, revealing your shadow, before you could become an initiate and move into the awakening process. Until you were willing to own up to the whole of who you were, you couldn't enter into the mystery.

Exercise: The Two-Faced Mask

This practice is a powerful way to unmask the shame you hide, befriend your shadow and step into your fully authentic self.

Step 1

- Buy a white plastic or paper mask like the one in Figure 3 (*see page 84*), or, if that's not possible, make yourself a mask out of paper or card. Get yourself some marker pens with which to write on the mask too.

- The final part of this exercise requires standing in front of a mirror, so make sure you have access to one.

Step 2

- Take a moment to come into an awareness of your breath. Just notice when you are breathing in and notice when you are breathing out.

- Notice three inhalations and exhalations before you begin.

- On the outside of the mask, write or depict all of the qualities that make up your persona - how you like to present yourself to the world. These may be true qualities, but they may also be aspirational ones or even just plain untrue.

Step 3

- On the inside of the mask, write or depict all of the seemingly shameful traits, habits, secrets, taboos and shadow aspects that you hide from others.

  If there is anything that you are absolutely unable to write down, feel free to represent it through a symbol or acronym that only you know the meaning of. But don't censor yourself – just go for it. You can't get this stuff wrong.

Step 4

- Once you have finished the inside of the mask, take some time to notice any correlations between the persona side and the shadow side. Do any qualities directly mirror each other or directly contradict each other?

Step 5

- Stand in front of a mirror and hold the mask up in front of your face with the persona side facing you.

- Read through (out loud if possible) all the aspects of your persona and just notice how each one makes you feel.

  Remind yourself that your persona is not wrong, it is just your preferred image of yourself. The persona is, as Robert Holden once told me, 'at best a pale photocopy of your true self and is nothing compared to how the divine sees you'.

Step 6

- Now flip the mask around so that the shadow side is facing you.

- Read through (out loud if possible) all the aspects of your shadow side and just notice how each one makes you feel.

  Shame derives its power from being unspeakable, so to declare our shame out loud is to strip it of its power and liberate ourselves from its stranglehold.

Step 7

- Finally, drop the mask. Literally drop it to the floor and stand looking at your original face in the mirror.

- Witness yourself with love.

- Say the following (out loud if possible), as you look at your original face in the mirror:

  I bear witness to my persona. I bear witness to my shadow.
  I send love to my persona. I send love to my shadow.
  I am more than my persona. I am more than my shadow.
  I am my original face. *

- Dedicate the beneficial energy of this exercise to all beings.

---

* The 'original face' is a term used in Zen Buddhism to point to the non-duality of subject and object.

Step 8 (optional)

Simply by bringing these hidden traits into the light of your awareness you have begun the integration process and diminished the power that these aspects used to have over you, but you might like to take the integration one step further.

- *Only if and when you feel ready to do so,* find a way to share your mask – both sides of it – with another person. This could be a close friend or therapist if you are currently seeing one.

- You might also like to upload a photo of your mask to the gallery on my Facebook page (Charlie Morley-Lucid Dreaming and Shadow Work) called 'Shadow masks'. You will find dozens there already and you will probably find at least a couple of your shadow traits listed on the masks there too.

For many people at my workshops, this is the most powerful exercise they do there. One lady called Maki, a computer skills tutor who had struggled with self-love, told me:

> It was amazing. It clarified so much for me and really helped me. At the end, when I dropped the mask and saw my own face, I felt real love for myself – acceptance and self-love. It was brief, but I felt it. It was very powerful and the feeling came back a few times in the following days too.

Once you start to do this work, you realize that everybody else is wearing a mask too and trying to maintain a façade. That's a great relief, because then you don't have to pretend as much. You can relax and be more open and honest with life. You can start to operate from a place of greater love and authenticity.

Now let's explore the other facets related to the persona and the shadow: ego and Buddha nature.

The Wizard of Ego

I've seen the film *The Wizard of Oz* literally dozens of times. This is because, along with *Grease* and *The African Queen*, it was the only VHS (just google it, millennials) that my grandma had.

Throughout the film the wizard is presented as a kind of omniscient god. When Dorothy and the other heroes first meet him, they are confronted by a huge face made of light beaming down at them, warning them how great and powerful he is. When they meet him again, though, after slaying the wicked witch, they find the great wizard is a tiny old man speaking into a megaphone and pulling frantically at the levers and light projectors he uses to create the godly face and booming voice. Perhaps most tellingly, even after his true nature is revealed, he continues to pull the levers and shine the lights in a desperate attempt to maintain his illusory power.

Our limited sense of self, sometimes called the ego, is a bit like the wizard: an ageing magician who keeps pulling the levers that maintain the illusion that it is the most powerful force in our mind.

Although the term 'ego' often has pejorative connotations, from a Buddhist point of view the problem is not our ego but our attachment to it and belief that it is the whole of us. The ego is just an incomplete and tragically limited rendering of who we really are.

So the ego is actually not the problem; egocentricity is.

Buddha Nature

In Tibetan Buddhism it is believed that the potential to attain complete spiritual awakening is present in the mindstream of every living being, from squid to Satanist. This potential is called Buddha nature and it means that we are all born not as sinners, but as Buddhas.*

Buddhist master Tai Situpa sums this up by saying, 'At an ultimate level, you are perfect, they are perfect, everyone is

---

* The term 'Buddha' often refers to Siddhartha Gautama, the man who pioneered the spiritual path that would later become known as Buddhism. More generally, though, 'buddha' can refer to anyone who has attained the state of complete spiritual awakening.

perfect. All of us have limitless potential ... the potential of everyone is perfect all the time.'[6]

Buddha nature reveals that we are, in fact, enlightened already. All the karma, concepts and emotional patterns of our shadow side are nothing more than clouds temporarily blocking the endless sunlight of our already enlightened mind. And, just like the sun behind the clouds, however hidden our Buddha nature may be, it is always there.

So why don't we recognize it?

Just as some people can spend hours gazing up at the clouds but no more than a couple of seconds looking into the blinding light of the sun, so we can gaze for whole lifetimes at the clouds of our emotional patterns, but not spend even a moment looking into our own Buddha nature.

As a consequence, we fail to recognize our original nature and 'instead, we take ourselves to be the ongoing stream of thoughts and emotions that arise moment to moment'[7] in the mind. We identify so strongly with our thoughts and habits that we solidify our sense of self around them. And so begins what I call 'the Great Forgetting'.

The Great Forgetting

It seems to be that underlying the unenlightened human condition is a self-defeating faith in our own limitations. The Buddhist masters say, 'This not only denies us all hope of awakening, but also tragically contradicts the central truth of Buddha's teaching: that we are all already essentially perfect.'[8]

We forget the purity of our own nature. We forget our true potential and identify instead with our ego and its self-attacking thoughts, thus 'abandoning our Buddha nature in favour of attachment to ourselves as a separate'[9] and most definitely non-enlightened being.

The whole purpose of the spiritual path is, as Buddhist master Dzogchen Ponlop Rinpoche says, 'to correct this misperception and uncover our self-existing wisdom'.[10] Not to kill off the ego, simply to give it a supporting role while our Buddha nature takes the lead.

Our fully awakened state is so magnificent in its power (and our experience of it so fleeting) that we view it as an altered state of consciousness when, in fact, it *is* consciousness. Perhaps the real altered state is the sleepy egocentricity of our everyday mind?

Exercise: The Good News and the Bad News

One of the best ways to meet the Wizard of Ego and remember our own Buddha nature is to ask those who love us what they think of us. Author of *Your Golden Shadow* William A. Miller says this is 'one of the most effective ways of gaining insight into our personal shadow'.[11]

Asking people what they think of us is a powerful and surprisingly energizing exercise, but fear around it is quite natural. I was terrified by it when I first came across it in Debbie Ford's *Dark Side of the Light Chasers*. I was afraid that I'd be told what I feared most, and be judged or insulted. And yet I knew that the spiritual path was based upon 'the willingness to abandon the habitual disposition of avoiding facing ourselves'[12] and so if I was serious about spiritual development, this exercise was a must.

In fact, what happened was a close encounter not only with how I was perceived by others, but also with all the golden potential that others saw and appreciated in me. I thought it was an exercise in dark shadow exposure, but I found out that it was actually a way of seeing my golden one.

I suggest doing this exercise with three separate loved ones. Loved ones are often in the best position to see our shadow sides and although doing this practice with an acquaintance might seem easier, it defeats one of the objects of the exercise: to move into places that scare you.

Step 1

- Feeling free to explain as much or as little about this exercise as you like, find some time to be alone with a loved one.

- Make sure they feel safe enough to speak freely and honestly. Explain to them that you will not be picking apart their answers, just listening to and witnessing their feedback.

Step 2

- Ask them what three things they like most about you. Ask them to be honest and open and feel free to say: 'Thank you, can you tell me a bit more about that?'

- If what they say seems too good to be true, don't reject your perceived brilliance, simply say: 'Thank you, can you tell me a bit more about that?'

- When they have finished, resist the urge to question them on their feedback or to defend yourself in anyway. Just thank them for being so honest and give them a hug or make some physical contact with them if possible.

Step 3

- Now, remind yourself that this exercise is showing you how you are *perceived* by others, not necessarily how you *actually are* and so there is no need to argue or defend yourself.

- Ask your loved one what three things they like least about you. Encourage them to be direct but gentle and feel free to say: 'Thank you, can you tell me a bit more about that?'

- If what they say hurts you, simply feel the feeling. If you need to, you can even say something like: 'Ouch, that one hurt, but please continue.'

- Once they have finished, resist the urge to question them on their feedback or to defend your ego. Simply thank them for being so honest and give them a hug or make some sort of physical contact with them if possible.

Step 4

- Finally, ask them to remind you of the three qualities they liked most about you. It's important to hear your most likeable qualities *again* before you finish.

- With the energy of these three qualities, let them know that the exercise is now over and that you are grateful to them for helping you uncover your shadow side.

- Take a moment to dedicate the beneficial energy of this exercise to yourself and to all living beings.

In Your Dreams...

> *'The reason that we all dream so much is that the dreamer wants to remind us of the amount of shadow that we haven't yet absorbed.'*
> **Robert Bly**[13]

Once you have established regular dream recall and started keeping a dream diary, you can begin recognizing and decoding the appearance of the shadow in your dreams.

We are working from the basis that everything in your dream is in some way a reflection of your own psychology, so if you dream about a particular person, focus more on what part of yourself they might *represent* rather than who they actually are in waking life.

From this perspective your dark shadow is quite easy to recognize – it is anything in a dream that makes you feel afraid, disgusted, ashamed or annoyed. Anything you would rather avoid (be it a situation or a person) is also a reflection of your dark shadow, as of course is anything in the dream that reflects the contents of your bag or the inside of your mask.

And the golden shadow? You've guessed it: any person or situation in the dream that you admire, idolize or venerate. Dreams of celebrities* or famous individuals, of flying or laughing or of joyful things or spiritual teachers all carry a heavy dose of the golden shadow for most people.

A guy on one of the six-week shadow courses felt that his shadow simply wasn't showing up in his dreams. I asked him if he'd noticed any changes in his dreams since he'd started the course and he said that he'd kept dreaming about the British prime minister, Theresa May. When I asked him what qualities she represented to him, he said, 'Steadiness, courage and strength.' As he spoke, his eyes lit up as he realized that those were three major traits on his golden shadow list!

Exercise: Recognizing the Shadow in Dreams

1. Set your intention to remember and recall your dreams as you fall asleep.

2. Upon awakening, recall and document your dreams in your dream diary. You don't have to write down every detail you'll know what feels worth noting, but be sure to capture the main themes and feelings and the general narrative of the dream.

3. Then once you've done so, ask yourself:

   - *'What are the dominant emotional themes of this dream?' For example, sadness, joy, searching, adventure.*

   - *'Do any people or scenarios in the dream reflect aspects of my dark shadow? If so, which?'*

   - *'Do any people or scenarios in the dream reflect aspects of my golden shadow? If so, which?'*

---

* Some people dream of having sex with celebrities. Sex in dreams is often used as a symbol for unity and for bringing together that which is separate. So, if you dream of having sex with a certain celebrity, ask yourself, 'What qualities within me does this celebrity represent?' because it may be that those qualities are currently being unified within you.

- *'Are there any figures in my dream that may be personifications of my personal shadow?' For example, celebrities, archetypal figures, animals.*

- *'What do I think the dream wants to highlight for me?'*

It takes time and practice to decode all the various shadow aspects in your dreams, but it's well worth doing. It's fascinating to see which aspects turn up and how they have been invoked by things you have suppressed, projected or acted out during the day.

To make a conscious effort to get in touch with the feeling of a dream (rather than just recalling its content) is to spend time hanging out with your unconscious, paying homage to its offerings and familiarizing yourself with your shadow.

Once you know what to look for, you'll soon find your shadow playing a central role (or at least making a cameo appearance) in many of your dreams. This is a good sign, as it shows that the shadow is ready to reveal itself and wants to be integrated.

Shaking Hands with My Inner Trump

In life, most of us don't want to face the shadow, so we deny it. In dreams, it can't be denied, because it's on its own territory. Knowing that we can't consciously avoid it, as we do when awake, it moves towards us, wanting to be known. The main thing of course is to face it and embrace it, however scary it may seem.

The night before the 2016 US Presidential Election, I went to sleep with some anxiety about the vote. That very night I had a dream about meeting Donald Trump.

> *We were in a town square in Ashland, Oregon, and I remember feeling both intrigued and hesitant about meeting him, as he was not a man whose policies I admired.*

He came over to me and asked me who I was voting for, and when I explained that I was British and couldn't vote in the US election, he was jovial and warm-hearted towards me. As he shook my hand, I remember feeling almost annoyed at how friendly and nice he seemed. He wasn't how I had expected him to be at all.

I woke up, wrote down the dream and used the Recognizing the Shadow in Dreams exercise to recognize and decode it. I asked myself, 'What parts of my dark shadow does Donald Trump represent to me? Xenophobia? Misogyny? Megalomania?' I felt embarrassed as I realized that as this was my dream, these were parts of my mind. And yet what was the dream highlighting for me? That these harmful and rejected parts of me were extending the hand of friendship. They wanted to be integrated. They needed my love, not my vitriol. Perhaps the same is true of Donald Trump?

CHAPTER 7

'NO MUD, NO LOTUS'

*'Be like a lotus. Let the beauty
of your heart speak.'*

Amit Ray[1]

In all the schools of Buddhism the lotus flower is a symbol of our innate enlightened potential. The reason for this stems from how the lotus grows.

Lotus seeds grow most readily in the deep sludge at the bottom of ponds. When they sprout, they are naturally attracted to the sunlight that shines down through the murky water and instinctively reach up to it, eventually blossoming above the surface of the water, untainted by the mud from whence they came, pristine, perfect and beautiful.

Buddhist thought tells us that the lotus flower is like our Buddha nature and the muddy pond is like our shadowy mind. All the dark, shameful, unacceptable aspects of both our mind and our life form the fertile mud in which the lotus can grow. Without the mud, there can be no lotus.

The first time I came across this concept, I was amazed to learn that rather than getting rid of my muddy, shadowy, seemingly 'negative' mind-states, I could *actively use* them for spiritual growth.

It's been said that 'suffering and awakening form a single weather-system'[2] and so we can be glad of our pain, for it opens our heart. This is great advice, but when we are knee-deep in the mud of our own suffering, it can be difficult to imagine a lotus growing there.

With time, though, we often come to realize that the pain we've experienced in our life has made us who we are and that if it hadn't been for that situation or heartbreak or redundancy or illness, we wouldn't have encountered the life opportunities that these led to. There is a Tibetan saying: 'Just as a bonfire in a strong wind is not blown out, but blazes even brighter, so too can our mind be strengthened by the difficult situations we encounter.'

This is not about spiritual bypassing and seeing 'the bright side', but simply about acknowledging how the mud of our suffering can often lead to spiritual growth.

To become a shadow worker is to become the gardener of our own mind, acknowledging that our shadow isn't something to get rid of, it is something that fertilizes the seeds of our own awakening.

The Science of Post-Traumatic Growth

The 'no mud, no lotus' concept has verification from mainstream psychology. Post-traumatic growth (PTG) is the phenomenon of positive change that is made through the experience of trauma and adversity. More than half of all trauma survivors actually report positive change.[3]

A 2009 British Journal of Health Psychology article reviewing the past 20 years of studies into PTG reported: 'The studies consistently found that their respondents had a new appreciation of life, calling it a "gift", and that they were "thankful" that they had been touched by such life-altering illnesses or events.'[4]

Psychologists agree that 'the acute period of depression, anxiety or nightmares caused by the trauma can be followed by arriving at an even higher level of psychological and emotional functioning than before the adversity'.[5]

Researchers commented how 'people said that despite the physical pain they suffered, the daily struggles they faced, their lives were unquestionably better today than before their traumatic experiences. Trauma sent them on a path they never would have found otherwise.'[6]

Exercise: Finding the Lotus in the Mud

This exercise, inspired by my friend and mindfulness teacher Fay Adams, asks you to find moments in your life when the mud of suffering led to the lotus of new growth, opportunity or insight.

When I first did this exercise, I thought back to the panic attacks that led me to find Buddhist meditation, the nightmares of my teens that led me to lucid dreaming and the heartbreak that led me to finally face myself.

At workshops people have shared how losing their job led them to the career they had always dreamed of, how mental breakdown led them to the spiritual path and how illness was the wake-up call that led to living a fuller life.

When in *your* life has the mud of suffering led to the blossoming of your potential?

1. Take a moment to come into an awareness of your breath. Just notice when you are breathing in and notice when you are breathing out. Notice three inhalations and exhalations before you begin.

2. Using Figure 4 (*see page 102*), or by making your own, write on the mud section any crisis points in your life or times of suffering (for example, illness, losing your job, a relationship breakdown) that you now see were either wake-up calls or that led to times of personal growth or benefit. Even if you can only think of one or two examples, that's fine.

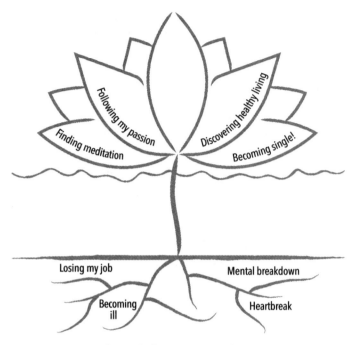

Figure 4: Create your own lotus

3. Write on the lotus petals the beneficial things that blossomed from the experiences that you had in the mud (for example, a new perspective on life, freedom, the opportunity to follow your passion).

4. Take a moment to think back to what happened and to appreciate and perhaps even to send love to the people or situations that created the mud.

5. Dedicate the beneficial energy of this exercise to all beings.

We all have dark shadows and golden ones and we are all ashamed to show some of them and too scared to acknowledge the power of others. So often we see ourselves as lonely victims among strangers who don't know our pain. But everyone has been through pain and suffering. And everyone has Buddha nature. Imagine if we could take time to really witness the mud that another person has been through as well as the lotus of awakening that is within them.

Exercise: Witnessing the Lotus

This exercise asks you to see the lotus and the mud in another person. It is inspired by an eye-gazing technique taught to me by my friend, philosopher Tim Freke, and it explores vulnerability, projection, empathy and Buddha nature.

Along with the mask exercise (see *page 87*), this is a firm favourite with participants at the workshops, and one young journalist even said it was one of the most powerful compassion exercises he had ever done. It's one of my personal favourites too, so I implore you not to skip it just because it requires a partner. Find someone, anyone, even a stranger if you like, but definitely be sure to do this exercise.

Because you and your partner will each have your eyes closed at different times, it is best done as a guided meditation. It can be found set to music and guided by my voice at www.charliemorley.com/shadowexercises under the title 'Witnessing the Lotus'. Or you can follow the steps below and record your own version to use.

Step 1

- Sit opposite your partner. Decide who is Person A and who is Person B.

- With your eyes closed, both of you take a moment to breathe and become aware of your body supported unconditionally by the chair or cushion beneath you.

- Your intention is to bear witness to your partner with compassionate awareness. To see them fully and completely. To witness both their mud and their lotus.

Step 2

- And now, Person A, open your eyes. Take a moment to bear witness to your partner. Take a moment to recognize the mud of their struggle. Just like you, they have known pain. Just like you, they have made mistakes. And just like you, they are trying their best. Hold them in your awareness for the next few moments.

- And now, Person A, close your eyes, and Person B, open your eyes. Person B, take a moment to bear witness to your partner. Take a moment to recognize the mud of their struggle. Just like you, they have known pain. Just like you, they have made mistakes. Just like you, they are trying their best. Hold them in your awareness for the next few moments.

- Now, Person B, close your eyes, and Person A, open your eyes. Person A, take a moment to bear witness to your partner. Take a moment to recognize the lotus of their true potential, their divine light, their Buddha nature. Just like you, they have enlightened potential. Just like you, they are ready to wake up. You are gazing upon a Buddha in the making, a lotus ready to bloom. Hold them in your awareness for the next few moments.

- Now, Person A, close your eyes, and Person B, open your eyes. Person B, take a moment to bear witness to your partner. Take a moment to recognize the lotus of their true potential, their divine light, their Buddha nature. Just like you, they have enlightened potential. Just like you, they are ready to wake up. You are gazing upon a Buddha in the making, a lotus ready to bloom. Hold them in your awareness for the next few moments.

- Person A, keep your eyes closed, and now Person B, close your eyes too.

Step 3

- Now that you have seen each other's mud and lotus, prepare to bear witness to the whole person, with compassionate awareness.

- Person A and Person B, open your eyes.

- Look into each other's eyes and bear witness to the Buddha that sits before you. You are dreamers in the same dream, both wanting love and both trying your best, both sleeping Buddhas slowly awakening to your full potential. See the Buddha in each other's eyes. Hold each other's gaze for the next few moments.

Step 4

- Take a moment to dedicate the beneficial energy that you have just generated to all living beings.

- Then find a way to thank your partner.

- Spend some time discussing your experience and reflecting on it.

In Your Dreams...

So far we have learned how to recall our dreams, diarize our dreams, infuse the hypnagogic state with golden shadow energy and recognize the shadow in our dreams – perfect preparation for the lucid dreaming practices that we will be exploring soon.

Now that we have a solid foundation, let's move on to something a bit more direct: calling the shadow into our dreams.

Exercise: Calling the Shadow into Your Dreams

Perhaps your shadow is already showing itself in your dreams, but if not, maybe it just needs some encouragement.

1. Lie down in bed, ready for sleep, and close your eyes. The aim of this practice is to stay in the hypnagogic state mindfully without entering into the sleep that lies beyond it.

2. As you drift into the hypnagogic state, recite one of the following statements over and over in your mind:

> *Shadow, come to me, I am ready to meet you!*
> *Shadow, show yourself – enter my dreams!*

3. After a few minutes of recitation, allow yourself to fall asleep, saturated with the energy and intention of your affirmation.

4. The next morning, or whenever you wake from your dreams, write them down and then go through the process of recognizing the shadow that we learned in the previous chapter (*see page 95*).

Personally, I've found that almost every time I ask for my shadow to appear in my dreams, it does appear – sometimes in a glaringly obvious form and other times in a form so subtle that it takes my wife, Jade, to point it out to me. She often knows my shadow far better than I do!

CHAPTER 8

REVOLUTIONIZING NIGHTMARES

*'With genuine self-acceptance and a
sense of humour we can uncover even
the darkest inner monsters with love.'*

Rob Preece[1]

Nightmares are some of the most tangible manifestations of the shadow and I've been fascinated by them since I was a child. Over the past 10 years I've worked with hundreds of nightmare sufferers, including armed forces veterans, victims of childhood abuse and even a survivor of a terrorist attack. What I've noticed is that for many of these people, the deepest healing has come from a shift of perspective concerning what nightmares actually signify. Once they recognize that they are a call for help rather than an attack by the unconscious, the road to healing opens up before them.

Many of us pathologize our nightmares as symptoms of a broken mind and so naturally try to get rid of them. In fact, nightmares are not only one of the most visceral ways to meet our shadow, but often also the sign of a mind that is healing itself.

A Dream That Is Shouting

Nightmares don't mean to hurt us, they mean to grab our attention. A nightmare is simply a dream that is shouting. It is shouting, 'Hey, look at this! Deal with this! This needs attention!'

If we are willing to embrace rather than reject our nightmares, we can foster a shift of perspective that tells them: 'I am ready to bear witness to you. I understand that you're an expression of my own mind that just wants to be seen.' And upon receiving that message, the shadow creating the nightmares might not feel the need to shout so loudly in future.

For the most part, people judge their nightmares as bad, and so they turn away from them or try to wake themselves from them. However, this leaves the energy of the nightmare unintegrated and, in many cases, leads to it recurring.

We need to revolutionize our view of nightmares. We need to stop seeing them as a sign of spiritual failure or a broken mind and start seeing them as creative responses to our own internal healing mechanism. In many cases having nightmares is a sign that our mind is ready to reveal and heal its shadow side and to integrate the energy that has been locked away for so long.

This new perspective may spill over into our waking life, too, and we may start to view nightmarish situations with new eyes and a new appreciation of the potential for healing that they offer us.

PTSD Shadow Work

In the summer of 2016 I was privileged to offer some teaching on lucid dreaming to a wonderful group of armed forces veterans as part of a mindfulness meditation retreat at Samye Ling Monastery in Scotland.

The course leader was a huge-hearted veteran of the Parachute Regiment called Keith McKenzie. Keith was a trained mindfulness teacher and had briefed me that many in the group had been diagnosed with post-traumatic stress disorder (PTSD), due to the horrors of the wars of which they had been part.

Post-traumatic stress disorder is a psychological condition that occurs after an extremely stressful event, such as physical violence or exposure to a warzone. Those suffering from it may have recurring memories of the stressful event and may feel anxious or scared even in the absence of danger. Flashbacks and nightmares are common symptoms as well.

Some of the stories these war veterans told and the nightmares they shared will be forever etched into my memory. These men and women bore their scars with a courage and dignity I hadn't dreamed possible.

Although I was with them for only two days and we worked mainly on the basics (hypnagogic meditation, reframing the perception of nightmares and the mechanics of sleep), our work together seemed to really benefit them.

The morning after our first workshop, one of the group came in beaming and told us, 'I did it – I slept through the night! Hasn't happened for months!' Another said that he had woken up 'feeling amazing' after a dream in which he was a golden eagle.

After the last session one veteran told me, 'This has given us a new circle. We used to have a circle of despair, but now we've got a circle of hope.'

Working with the veterans gave me renewed appreciation of just how awful the recurring nightmares of PTSD can be and also new appreciation of the healing potential of dream work.

Justin Havens, a psychological therapist conducting PhD research into the PTSD nightmares of veterans at Anglia Ruskin University in the UK, agrees that nightmares are signs of healing. He told me that current psychological research has shown that 'when bad things happen we are supposed to dream about them, because the nightmare is highlighting a problematic aspect such as unresolved emotional distress that needs to be integrated'.[2]

He went on to say that waking ourselves from a nightmare was to be avoided because it prevented the dream content from being fully integrated and told me about one of the most exciting cutting-edge treatments for nightmares: Planned Dream Intervention. This is an approach that aims to teach the brain at an unconscious level that there is no such thing as a bad dream and that whatever a dream presents us with is to be witnessed with acceptance.

The Science of Lucid Dreaming for PTSD

Lucid dreaming is one of the most effective treatments for the nightmares that are often symptomatic of PTSD.

A 1997 study that took five people suffering from chronic nightmares and taught them to lucid dream concluded that 'the alleviation of recurrent nightmares was effective in all five cases' and that 'treatments based on lucid dream induction can be of therapeutic value'.[3]

A follow-up study one year later showed that 'four of the five subjects no longer had nightmares and that the other experienced a decrease in the intensity and frequency of her nightmares'.[4]

A 2006 study entitled 'Lucid Dreaming for Treatment of Nightmares' concluded that 'lucid dream training seems effective in reducing nightmare frequency'[5] and at the 2009 European Science Foundation meeting it was stated that lucid dreaming was such an effective remedy for nightmares that people had the potential to be 'treated by training to dream lucidly'.[6]

And finally, a 2013 neurobiological study from Brazil concluded that lucid dreaming could be used 'as a therapy for post-traumatic stress disorder'.[7]

Signs of a Healing Mind

It was from her lowest point that her breakthrough came. I found her wandering the apartment at 2 a.m., repeating over and over, 'The dreams, Charlie, the dreams…'

The day before I had had a very direct, perhaps too direct, conversation with my mum about her diagnosis of early-onset Alzheimer's disease. I was trying, however clumsily, to help her accept her condition and move out of the denial stage that she had been in for months.

She was, and still is, a vivacious, glamorous woman who took the diagnosis in her stride and kept on embracing life, but she was unwilling to discuss the diagnosis openly or share it with even her closest friends. This was ringing alarm bells for me, but it was actually the fact that she hadn't had any anxiety dreams or nightmares since her diagnosis that was most alarming. We'd been sharing our dreams for years, so I was well acquainted with her dream life, and I was concerned that her repression was so deep that it was operating at the level of dreaming too.

I'm not suggesting that we have to have nightmares to heal, but for healing to occur, the mind does have to process grief, either in the waking state through mourning and talking and reflection, or through dreams, or very often both. My mum wasn't doing either and I knew it was probably indicative of a mind that wasn't moving through the integration process. And so I was direct with her about the facts, almost but not quite regrettably so, as I attempted to help her move out of the denial stage that she was so obviously still in.

That night the nightmares came. Her mind was finally processing her grief. To comfort her I slept in her bed next to her, just as she used to do with me when I had nightmares as a child. As I lay there watching her sleep and wrestling with the guilt I was feeling, I realized that our roles had become reversed, as so often they do when our parents get older, and that now

I would stand guard as she slept, ready to slay dragons for her, just as she had done for me.

Eventually I slipped into sleep myself and into the inevitable guilt-ridden anxiety dreams that I knew I needed to face.

The next morning she was different. Something had shifted. As we discussed the nightmares, laughed about our 2 a.m. run-in and spoke openly for the first time about her feelings of despair, I knew that her mind was moving out of denial and towards acceptance. We started discussing bucket-list adventures and plans for the future. Eventually she started to open up to her friends about it too.

Although that night was horrific for my mum, and I still carry some shadows of guilt from it, it was when she finally faced her demons that she truly started to heal.

The Science of Sleep Paralysis

No chapter on nightmares would be complete without at least touching on sleep paralysis. For many people, this phenomenon – of partially waking from sleep but the body remaining paralysed – is a terrifying experience in which hallucinatory images and sounds may lead them to believe that demons are trying to possess them.

Sleep paralysis most commonly occurs during the hypnopompic state (the transitional state of waking from sleep and dream), but sometimes in the hypnagogic, too. It is caused by one of the three REM dreaming sleep systems (muscular paralysis),* staying engaged when the other two (sensory blockade and cortical activation) have been disengaged, meaning that while our brain has partially woken up and our senses are taking in partial sensory input, our physical body cannot move.

---

* The brain paralyses the body during REM dreaming sleep as a safety precaution to stop us acting out our dreams.

Due to the brain's momentary engagement in both the dream state and waking state, there may be hallucinatory images superimposed over the normal field of vision; there are often loud audio hallucinations too. The fear that this altered state generates can also lead to hyperventilation, and in turn a feeling of weight on the chest.

The best way to break free from sleep paralysis is to relax and exhale through your front teeth, making a sound similar to letting air out of a tyre. This relaxation of the respiratory system will help to disengage the paralysis mechanism. Or, if you're feeling brave, try to stay with it and you might find that it transforms into a lucid dream.

Energetic Potential

I want you to imagine two dreams. In dream number one you're walking down the street with a friend. In dream number two you're being chased by axe-wielding zombie maniacs. Which is the 'bad dream'?

Most people will say the second, because you're being chased and in danger. However, which dream has the more energy? The energetic potential of the second dream is way higher than that of the first dream and so its potential for integrating shadow energy is far greater too.

Nightmares are expressions of energy, not evil. The energy powering them has been lying dormant and unintegrated, but now it's being displayed. And simply by being displayed, it's being integrated at some level.

We can help this process along by embracing our nightmares with acceptance, friendliness and kindness. Acceptance involves writing the dream down and bearing witness to its shadow content.*

---

* Definitely write down your nightmares. If you like, you can draw them, paint them or write poems about them. Why? Because you want to do everything you can to tell the nightmare, 'Okay, I'm listening. There's no need to keep shouting!'

Then, by learning how to become lucid within it, we can befriend and show kindness to the shadow aspect that the axe-wielding zombie maniacs represent.

The fruition of this shift of perspective is that we can get to a point where we can actually be excited about having a nightmare, knowing that its energetic potential is far greater than that of most everyday dreams.

In the next chapter we're going to explore integrating shadow energy through lucid dreaming, but before that let's look at two great exercises for anyone suffering from the fear that nightmares can often unwittingly cause.

Exercise: The 4, 7, 8 Breath

It's 4 a.m. and you've just woken up from a nightmare. You're feeling shaken and can't get back to sleep. Or maybe you've been in bed for hours, lying awake because you're scared of having a nightmare. You need the 4,7,8 breath.

This is a form of *pranayama* (breath control) from the ancient yogic system of India, but it's the American Dr Andy Weil, founder of the Arizona Center for Integrative Medicine, who has conducted the most conclusive research into its effects. He says, 'This is a great way to help you fall asleep. Or if you wake up in the middle of the night and can't get back to sleep, this technique will help you fall asleep right away.'[8]

The 4,7,8 breath is a natural tranquillizer for the nervous system. But unlike tranquillizing drugs, which often lose their power over time, this exercise gains in power with repetition and practice.

1. Sitting on your bed, ready for sleep, place your tongue behind your upper front teeth and exhale completely and audibly through your mouth.

2. Now close your mouth and inhale through your nose for a count of four.

3. Hold your breath for a count of seven.

4. Release your breath through your mouth audibly for a count of eight.

Repeat this process four times for the first few times you do it, then increase your repetitions as you like up to 12 times.

―――――――――――――

In Your Dreams...

Shadow work isn't meant to be scary, but sometimes our ego can make it feel as though it is, especially if we're about to delve deep into our nightmares. If ever you feel a bit scared or anxious before sleep, the next meditation is what you need.

Exercise: The Circle of Allies

This is a visualization practice in which we imagine a gathering of allies around us, fearlessly supporting our shadow work and standing guard over us as we sleep.

This practice is inspired by the Tibetan dream yoga teachings* in which it is said that if you are feeling anxious before you sleep, you should turn your sleeping area into a sacred protected space by imagining that you are surrounded by enlightened beings and *dakinis* (female embodiments of awakening) who remain 'like mothers watching over a child or guardians surrounding a king or queen'.[9]

Who should you visualize as your allies and protectors? Anyone or anything who offers you a feeling of love, safety, allegiance and protection. Your protectors can be living or dead, real or unreal, known or unknown. Personally, I imagine Lama Yeshe Rinpoche (my Buddhist master), Rob Nairn (my meditation teacher), Akong Rinpoche (my deceased teacher) and Padamsambhava (a powerful

―――――――――――――

* The lucid dreaming practices found within Tibetan Buddhism are referred to as dream yoga. Yoga means 'union', and dream yoga is about unifying the mind within our dreams.

Tantric master) in the four cardinal directions (north, south, east and west) and then I fill the gaps with other imagined spiritual beings or buddhas. Some people I've taught this to fall asleep imagining a buffalo, Jesus, a ball of white light and Gandalf, the wizard from *The Lord of the Rings*, standing guard. Be creative. There are no rules for this – you can't get it wrong.

I find that invoking an imagined gathering of my allies is a powerful preparation not only for sleep, but for whichever exercise or meditation I am about to do, so don't feel limited to bedtime when engaging this technique.

1. Lying in bed before sleep, decide which allies and protectors you are going to invoke.

2. Imagine that they are surrounding you. You might like to imagine four principal allies standing to the north, south, east and west of you.

3. Feel free to fill the gaps with as many others as you like so that eventually you are surrounded by love and protection.

4. Either fall asleep bathed in this atmosphere of protection or move into the first stage of any other dreamwork exercise you might be doing.

At an ultimate level, this exercise is, however, superfluous. Partly because there is nothing in your mind that you need to be protected from and partly because your allies are with you at all times anyway. They have never left your side, not once. In fact, this exercise doesn't as much call them in as open your eyes to see them there.

CHAPTER 9

LUCIDLY EMBRACING THE SHADOW

'Once lucid, there is no need to run from what you fear. Why run from it when you can transform it?'

Lama Yeshe Rinpoche[1]

I'm feeling excited as I write this. We are about to explore what I believe to be one of the most powerful psychological integration techniques there is. Through this method we will learn to call forth and integrate a personification of our own shadow in the amazing virtual reality of a lucid dream.

We can, as we've learned already, connect deeply with the shadow through contemplation, meditation and imagination exercises, but however deeply we may have gone into these practices, it would be very rare to encounter a seemingly physical manifestation of the shadow standing in front of us in one of them. In a lucid dream, though, that is exactly what can happen.

Lucid Dreaming

Those of you who have read my first two books will know all about this, but for those who haven't, let's explore the wonderful world of lucid dreaming.

Have you ever been in a dream and suddenly realized you are dreaming? That's called a lucid dream: a dream in which you are actively aware that you are dreaming as the dream is happening. You're sound asleep but have become fully conscious in the dream, totally aware that you're inside a 3D projection of your own mind. Once you know you're dreaming, you can, with practice, learn to direct the dream at will, all while you're sound asleep.

The Science of Lucidity

Lucid dreaming has been a scientifically verified phenomenon for over 40 years. In a more recent 2009 study, neurologists at Frankfurt University in Germany classified it as 'a hybrid state of consciousness'[2] in which areas of the prefrontal cortex (where rational thought and self-awareness arise) become activated while we're dreaming, which leads to self-awareness within the REM dream state.

Using brain-imaging technology such as magnetic resonance tomography and EEG, scientists can now pinpoint the actual 'Aha! I'm dreaming!' moment of lucid awareness and its neurophysiological correlates. In 2012, at Munich's Max Planck Institute of Psychiatry, it was discovered that when lucid consciousness was attained within the dream, activity in 'brain areas associated with self-assessment and self-perception, including the right dorsolateral prefrontal cortex and frontopolar regions, increase markedly within seconds'.[3]

This means the apparent paradox of being both aware and asleep, which had previously caused a lot of resistance and scepticism from the scientific establishment, was simply a failure to understand how two distinct brain regions could be activated simultaneously.

Fully lucid dreams can feel as real as waking life. In fact, they're so realistic that our brain functions as if we're awake and happily lays down neural pathways, which scientists have proven allows us to learn and get better at things that we practise in a lucid dream. Studies from Heidelberg University have shown that athletes who intentionally practised their athletic discipline in their lucid dreams actually got better at it in the waking state.[4] The fact that the brain's neural pathways can be affected during lucid dreaming means that overcoming a fear, moving through a psychological block or integrating a shadow aspect in a lucid dream isn't like dreaming it, it's like *doing* it, and can make lasting changes to the habits of our waking mind.

There are so many benefits to lucid dreaming, but in a nutshell, once we become conscious within our unconscious mind, we can optimize the functioning of our body and mind while we sleep.

Apart from meeting our shadow, a few of my favourite benefits of lucid dreaming are:

- exploring the unconscious (you are literally walking around a huge virtual-reality simulation of your own mind)

- engaging in spiritual practice while asleep (this is the main aim of Tibetan dream yoga)

- physical healing (a very powerful placebo effect can be engaged from within the lucid dream)

- asking questions/problem-solving (the unconscious has access to huge amounts of data, which makes it a great place for creative thinking)

- integrating the inner child (psychological integration of childhood trauma can be effected by invoking and embracing the archetype of the inner child)

Once lucid, we have the ability to interact with the dream and co-create the narrative. We can choreograph our dream experience, calling out for what we would like to happen and intentionally healing parts of our mind from within.

We don't control the dream, though, we simply orchestrate it: 'No sailor controls the sea. Similarly, no lucid dreamer controls the dream.'[5] Just as it would be an arrogant sailor who believed that they were controlling the awesome power of the sea, so it is with our dreams.

Let's not be arrogant sailors. We can't control the power of the unconscious mind, but what we can do is make friends with it, dialogue with it and finally start embracing the powerful energy it has been offering us every night of our life.

You've already covered the first two steps towards lucid dreaming: dream recall and keeping a dream diary. Appendix I (see page 221) will give you the rest of the steps you need. It can take a while to learn lucid dreaming, so if you're new to it, I recommend getting stuck into these techniques as soon as you can.

More important than all the techniques, though, are determination and enthusiasm. If you're feeling enthused about getting lucid and are determined to do it, there's no reason why you can't get started tonight.

Shadow Lucidity: The Three Options

In a lucid dream there are three main ways for us to interact with our shadow:

- The first is simply to bear witness to any shadow aspects that may already be present in the lucid dream. Simply bearing witness to them with love (or at least friendly curiosity rather than aversion) will integrate their underlying energy.

- The second is to proactively embrace them. If we see a disgusting or scary-looking dream character (fear or disgust being key indicators of shadow material), we can actually move towards them in the lucid dream and hug them – a hug being the ultimate symbolic expression of full acceptance.

• If the source of the shadow manifests as a situation rather than a person (such as a warzone or traumatic scenario), then our loving acceptance can be engaged by calling out statements such as: 'I integrate this shadow with love! I am free of this trauma!'

• And then there's the third option: to call forth our shadow aspects intentionally. Once lucid, we intentionally call forth the shadow in order to bear witness to it or dialogue with it (perhaps asking, 'What do you represent?'), and in all cases to embrace it with love. I'm sure you know the rules by now: face it, hug it, love it. If you can do that, you have the potential to, as a Jungian psychologist on one of my retreats once told me, 'do more in one lucid dream than you could do in years of therapy'.

Taming the Tiger

In the Tibetan dream yoga teachings, lucid dreaming is ultimately used to prepare for enlightenment, but the first thing we are advised to do once lucid is to transform fear. With fear being one of the biggest obstacles on the spiritual path (and yet often the hardest to see), any practices that we can use to transmute it are to be recommended.

The dream yoga teachings explain that once we're lucid, we should intentionally do things that scare us as a way of transforming fear and releasing the energetic blocks it so often creates. They specifically mention things like invoking a tiger so that we can 'jump into its mouth, ride on its back and even make friends with it'.[6]

If we can train in fearlessness in our dreams and nightmares, we can create a habit of courageous calm, rather than fear and panic, which will be a huge benefit to us not only in our daily life, but also in the after-death states. It's said that if you want to know how your mind will be at death, look at how your mind is during dreams. Lama Yeshe Rinpoche once told me, 'In dreams your fear can become 100 times more powerful, but in death it can become 1,000 times more powerful! We must train in fearlessness in our dreams to prepare to be fearless in death.'[7] (More about that in our final chapter.)

The teachings of traditional Tibetan medicine support this aspect of dream yoga training, as they too recommend that whenever anything of a threatening or nightmarish nature occurs in our dreams, such as being burned by fire, we should become lucid and 'jump fearlessly into the fire'[8] as a way of facing our fears, seeing the illusory nature of the dream and, again, preparing for death.

Fearless in the Waking Dream

This training in fearlessness doesn't just affect our dream life, it affects our waking life too. The Tibetan dream yogis say that when we become aware of our dreams we will start 'waking up to our delusory thoughts while we are awake … we will stop being duped by our projections'.[9] So much of our shadow is hidden beneath projection, but dream work directly helps to expose this.

We live as we dream, and so every time we embrace a shadow in a lucid dream, we create a habitual tendency to do the same while awake.

Lucid dreaming thus leads to lucid living. Every time we fly through the sky in a lucid dream, we are creating a new mental habit of moving beyond limitation in our waking life. Every time we embrace a shadow aspect in a lucid dream, we are creating a new habit in our waking life that says, 'I am no longer limited by fear.' Every time we walk through a wall in a lucid dream, we are engaging a new mindset that says, 'What seems to be solid is not always so.' With that, we are empowered to walk through the brick walls of our own bullshit when we wake up.

We sleep for a third of our life and through lucid dreaming we can use that third to train our mind to integrate our shadow, chose love over fear and manifest our highest potential during the two-thirds in which we are awake.

Dreaming through Darkness: My Journey into the Shadow

As part of the research for this book I wanted to chart my relationship with my shadow through my lucid dreams, so I read through every dream in every one of my dream diaries for the past 13 years. How had my relationship with my shadow developed over that time?

I'd been lucid dreaming since I was a teenager, but the first time I intentionally embraced my shadow in a lucid dream was over 10 years ago, when I was 23 years old.*

At that time I'd only just met Rob Nairn and to try to impress him I'd been boasting about how whenever anything dark or threatening appeared in my lucid dreams, I'd turn myself into a huge warrior and chop the threat to pieces so that I could carry on meditating in the dream as a 'good Buddhist' should.

He laughed at my naivety and said, 'Charlie, I advise you to do precisely the opposite of what you have been doing. This dark thing that you fear is your shadow. You must embrace your shadow.'

I was too embarrassed to say that I didn't know what the shadow was, so I googled it and read a few articles about it. Then two weeks later I got the chance to put Rob's advice into action.

---

* I talk about this experience in my 2013 TED talk, which you can find on YouTube.

I had become lucid and was about to start meditating and chanting mantras when a feeling of dread and fear enveloped me. Suddenly a shadow aspect made up of a three-headed monster moved forward to attack me.

I remembered Rob's advice, so I lunged at it and hugged it. It was a strong bear hug and it fought against it, but I held on tightly, trusting the advice of my teacher and somehow knowing that this seemingly paradoxical approach might just be the key to overcoming the monster.

It started to shrink in my arms and when I released the embrace, I found it had transformed into me. We stood looking into each other's eyes and I realized that I was looking at myself, maybe for the first time in my life.

When I told Rob about this and asked him if I had indeed embraced my shadow, he replied, laughing, 'Yes, absolutely. But "embrace the shadow" is a metaphorical term. I didn't mean for you to literally hug the thing, but hey, it worked!'

Over the past 10 years I've invoked and hugged literally dozens of shadow aspects in the form of mobsters, the devil, scenarios of doom and a whole load of zombies, knowing that in the symbolic landscape of the dream, a hug is the greatest symbol of love and acceptance.

My shadow has never appeared in a lucid dream the same way twice. But, whether as a hell's angel biker, a vampire, a transsexual Frenchman, a huge monster or the largest snake I could ever have dreamed of, it has given me a unique insight into the various aspects of myself – sexual, violent, judgemental or fear-based – that I have been unwilling to love at various times in my life.

If you're interested, you can check out one of my most interesting shadow lucid dreams, in which I met the essence of my shadow (see page 236).

Let's explore a couple of case studies now from people who have taught themselves to lucid dream using the techniques found in this book and learned how to meet their shadow in their dreams.

Meeting Sin

When a devoted Christian law student called Anthony met his shadow in a lucid dream, it appeared not as a monster but as the embodiment of sin itself. Anthony told me:

I had never heard of integrating shadow aspects in a lucid dream until I watched your TED talk. Up till then I had been using my lucid dreams to focus on my Christian practices like prayer and worship, but one night my shadow came to me.

I was having a nightmare set in my grandmother's house and a demon-like figure came down the hallway. It had a completely black body with no real shape to it, but it had a bright red face with bright red eyes.

The fear made me become lucid and, knowing that it must be a shadow aspect, I decided to confront it.

I asked it, 'What do you represent?'

And in a deep, booming voice, it replied, 'I am your sin!' and then it began to laugh.

I could almost feel it feeding off the aggression that I had confronted it with. Then I remembered you saying that you should hug your shadow.

Weirdly, the moment I decided to try to hug it, the demon started to back away from me, almost as though it knew what I was going to try to do. It backed into a corner, and as

I hugged it, it struggled in my arms and continued to laugh, mocking me almost.

I kept hugging it, though, and its laugh faded, as if it was losing energy. Then it just stopped. I looked into my arms and it was gone. The demon had dissolved into light. Everything became light.

The fear completely dissipated and the dream was still and quiet. When I woke up, I felt an amazing sense of peace.

Not only is that a brilliant example of shadow integration, but it also had a lasting effect on the dreamer. Anthony wanted to go on the record as saying, 'For anyone who says that your teachings are only for Buddhists, tell them that's just not true. Anyone, no matter what belief system they hold, can use lucid dreaming for their spiritual practice and to help themselves integrate their shadow.'

Her Seven-Year-Old Self

Just as we can integrate the shadow of our sin, so we can integrate the shadow created by what the Bible might describe as 'those who have sinned against us'.

A young lady on one of my lucid dreaming retreats decided that she wanted to meet her seven-year-old self in a lucid dream. She had never been lucid before, so I was curious as to why this was her plan. She explained that she had suffered emotional and physical abuse at this age and had carried a sense of guilt ever since. She wanted to meet her seven-year-old self in the lucid dream and tell her that it wasn't her fault and that she needn't feel guilty or be afraid anymore.

I was concerned that perhaps this was too sensitive a subject to explore in her first lucid dream and part of me was worried that she might unlock trauma from her past that shouldn't be tampered with. However, I trusted in the proven functionality of the shadow (it will only show you what you are ready for) and the innate intelligence of the unconscious mind, which always strives for harmonious balance within the psyche. I knew that if the unconscious didn't want her to become lucid, there was no way she could force the process.

That night she applied the lucidity techniques, became fully lucid and called out to meet her seven-year-old self. Fascinatingly, the intelligent self-regulation mechanism of the unconscious actually blocked her request (perhaps feeling that this might be too much for her to handle?) and no little girl appeared. Instead, the dream presented her with a door carrying a sign that said: 'Caution.' The shadow not only knew just what she was ready for, it even gave her a choice: you can open this door, but if you do, proceed with caution.

She did open the door and entered a building with many floors. On each floor was a different symbolic representation of the abuse, which she was then able to witness with loving acceptance. It was a deeply healing experience and it was a privilege to hear about it in the dream circle the next morning.

This example shows that when you call out to meet your shadow in a lucid dream, no dangerous floodgates swing open. Instead, a precise amount of shadow material is released by the intelligence of the dreaming mind.

Is It Always Our Dark Shadow?

Some dreamers fight their shadow aspects, as I used to, believing them to be harmful or even external forces that need to be destroyed. Why is this?

First, when we meet our shadow in lucid dreams, the degree to which we have befriended it will dictate how familiar it feels to us. Those with lesser integrated shadow sides may find it very hard to accept that the shadow aspect is them and not some 'dark energy' that has hacked into their dream.*

Secondly, because meeting our shadow forces us to witness the parts of ourselves that we are scared of, it's much easier to divert responsibility for our own darkness onto an external force.

Often when people meet angelic aspects in their lucid dreams, they're happy to accept them as their 'inner guides', but when a demonic aspect turns up, they're much less likely to accept it as part of themselves. They then misinterpret the shadow as some sort of evil or demonic presence that's both separate from them and harmful, and waste the valuable learning process it offers by investing their energy in ways to defeat it.

The truth is that the shadow is neither external nor harmful. It is part of us. Once we realize this, we can drop the fear-based paradigm of 'dark entities' hacking into our dreams and start to take responsibility for our own minds.

In Your Dreams...

As I mentioned earlier, if you want to learn how to lucid dream, then Appendix I (see *page 221*) covers all the basics. The exercise below requires you to lucid dream, so if you can't do it yet and want to skip ahead, that's fine, but I would recommend still reading through it, as it will help plant the seeds of lucidity in your mind.

---

* From a Buddhist point of view, in the lucid dream state we are actually in a stronger, more powerful state of mind than the waking state, as it is said that our lucid dreaming mind is up to seven times more powerful than our waking mind. This then begs the question: if 'negative energies' did want to hack into our mind, wouldn't they choose an easier time to do so?

Exercise: Lucid Dream Shadow Integration

1. Begin by creating a dream plan (*see page 231*) for meeting your shadow.

2. Engage your chosen lucid dreaming techniques (*see page 221*).

3. The next time you are lucid in your dreams, engage your dream plan by calling out your statement of intent, for example:

   Shadow, come to me!*

4. Sometimes the shadow will manifest obviously, as a personification, or an animal or monster, but other times it may come in subtler forms, for example as a rush of energy. Whatever manifests, actively embrace the shadow with acceptance. This could be by literally hugging it or by sending it your acceptance through affirming:

   I see you. I accept you. I am ready to embrace you!

   Essentially, it's about doing the opposite of what we usually do when we meet our dream shadow, which is to run from it, fight it or wake ourselves up from it.

   Whatever happens, you can't get this wrong. Simply by having the courage to meet your shadow, you are sending a powerful message that says, 'I am ready to meet you. I am ready to be friends.'

5. In the waking state, try to locate exactly what qualities were represented by whatever may have appeared to you as your shadow, for example aggression, repressed sexuality or trauma, and then explore how to continue integrating them in your waking life.

Not getting lucid yet?

For those of you who aren't able to lucid dream yet, I still advise going through the dream-planning process (*see page 231*). Also, why not try acting out your

---

*   In most cases, unless you specify that you particularly want to meet your golden shadow aspect, what appears usually contains predominantly dark shadow traits. My theory on why this should be is that the dark shadow contains an energy that is more readily available in the dream state, due to its long-term relationship to the creation of our nightmares. That's just a theory though.

dream plan in the dreamy space of the hypnagogic state instead? It may not be as direct and all-encompassing as the full HD realism of the lucid dream state, but it can be a powerful way to explore meeting your shadow in the interim.

CHAPTER 10

GOLDEN SHADOW LUCIDITY

*'You are not you. You are God forgotten
herself, dreaming that she is you.'*

Karma Dhonyo Drubpa

Imagine if you could meet a personification of your untapped potential. Imagine if you could have a dialogue with a representation of your hidden strengths. Imagine if you could actually hug your golden shadow. You can do all of this in your lucid dreams.

Until quite recently I'd never even considered the possibility of meeting my golden shadow in a lucid dream. Just over two years ago I tried it for the first time and discovered one of the most inspiring dream practices I've ever come across.

Experiments in a Goldmine

When I first tried this technique, I was still using the term 'positive shadow' (which is okay, but I find it a bit of a polarizing term), so one night I became lucid in my dream, remembered my intention and then called out, 'Positive shadow, come to me! I want to meet my positive shadow!' I had no idea what would happen next.

I guess I was expecting a personification of my positive shadow, maybe an angel or a wise man, to walk into the dream, but nothing really happened, so I decided to look around, still calling out my request.

Then I noticed a mirror hanging on a wall and in it I saw a reflection that wasn't mine. It was that of an older man, in his early sixties maybe, with a well-kept grey beard. He was smiling at me. He looked very familiar, but I couldn't quite place him.

I thought to myself, How does this guy relate to my positive shadow? And why does he look so familiar?

And then it hit me: it was me. An older version of me. I was looking at my future self.

To see him smiling at me was so moving. As we gazed at each other, I began to cry. I wondered whether this would be the age at which I integrated my shadow fully.

I then left the mirror and, still fully lucid, called out again, 'Positive shadow, come to me! I want to meet my positive shadow!'

This time something even more interesting happened.

A character walked in who was about my age, quite fat and looked a bit like The Simpsons *cartoon character called Comic Book Guy. He looked like a stereotypical video-game geek and he was wearing an ill-fitting retro T-shirt with a unicorn and a white shaggy dog on it.*

I started to think that maybe he was a personification of my inner geek and the part of me who was beyond body image, so I asked him, 'Are you my positive shadow?'

He replied, 'Me? No, I'm not. But look at this,' and he stretched out his T-shirt to display the unicorn and the white dog.

I said, 'Oh, I see! Is my positive shadow the unicorn?'

'No, not the unicorn, the dog!' he replied.

'The dog?' I asked.

'Yes! It's Arthur! Arthur the dog!' he chuckled.

I couldn't remember who Arthur the dog was and almost dismissed it, but when I woke up and googled his name, I was reminded why we should never dismiss what a lucid dream tells us.

Arthur the Dog

There is a sport called adventure racing in which teams of athletes take part in a race that lasts anything from three to eight days. During this time the teams will run, cycle, climb and kayak over hundreds of miles in some of the least hospitable areas of the planet, all against the clock.

In one well-documented story, a Swedish team racing in Ecuador as part of the World Championships picked up a new team-mate in the form of a stray and wounded dog they named Arthur. Arthur followed the team for days as they climbed up cliffs, trekked through the jungle and scrambled down ravines. He even swam beside their kayaks as they raced towards the finish. Never giving up despite his growing injuries, he actually crossed the finish line with the team some 100 miles later.

One member of the team, Mikael Lindnord, was so moved by the incredible bravery, endurance and tenacity of Arthur that he went through the nightmare of Ecuadorian bureaucracy to get him quarantined and flown back to Stockholm with him.[1] Their story has even been turned into a book – *Arthur: The Dog Who Crossed the Jungle to Find a Home.*

But how does all this relate to my golden shadow? When I first read about Arthur in the news, I was moved to tears. There was something about the loyalty, strength, love and, more than anything else, courage of that wounded stray dog that stuck with me. And it seems that it also stuck 'in' me too, as my dreaming mind chose Arthur to represent those qualities of my golden shadow.

Going for Gold

Since that first meeting I've called out to meet my golden shadow many more times and on each occasion I've been presented with a different symbolic representation of the untapped potential within me. One time it appeared as a person I often refer to as an angel because of a remarkable kindness she once showed me and another time as a group of smiling Tibetan monks – a symbol of my Buddha nature perhaps?

People I have taught this technique to have reported their golden shadow appearing as a mermaid (a symbol of beauty, enchantment and the water element?), a phoenix (a symbol of resurrection, power and the fire element?) and a bright white light that filled the entire dream.

To be able to touch, talk to and embrace a representation of your highest potential in the absolute HD clarity of a lucid dream is an unforgettable experience and highly beneficial for your psycho-spiritual growth.

Before we look at exactly how to do this, let's explore another way to embrace our golden shadow through lucid dreaming: by invoking a golden shadow archetype.

Golden Shadow Archetypes

Just as we have created external gods through the collective projection of our unmanifested divine potential, so we have created internal archetypes of our golden shadow too. Through lucid dreaming we can invoke these archetypes simply by calling them by name and integrate them by embracing them. If we call out for and then embrace HH the Dalai Lama, for example, we are integrating the golden spiritual potential that he might represent within ourselves.*

So who represents your golden potential – a saint, teacher, evolved being or even a well-loved celebrity? For me it was the 14th-century Persian poet Hafiz.

My Love Affair with Hafiz

When I encountered Hafiz, my life changed. His words struck chords within my heart that deafened self-doubt and left my Buddha nature ringing with joy. If I were to let myself write freely, there would be a whole chapter devoted to Hafiz and the power of his poetry, but for now let me share some of the words that touched me so deeply.

Through the skilful translation of Daniel Ladinsky, Hafiz perfectly sums up seeing the Buddha nature in another:

> I wish I could show you,
> When you are lonely or in darkness,
> The astonishing light of your own being.[2]

And he is aware of the infinite joy that resides within us once we integrate the shadow fully:

---

* Is it always our golden shadow, though? Could it be that we are, say, actually meeting the Dalai Lama? It is possible, but to believe that this is always the case may actually be disempowering, because it concretizes the unconscious belief that we don't have such spiritual potential within us.

I am happy even before I have a reason.
I am full of Light even before the sky
Can greet the sun or the moon.
Dear companions,
We have been in love with God
For so very, very long.
What can Hafiz now do but Forever
Dance!³

The more of his work I read, the more my heart opened, until I was verging on an obsessive hunger for his poetry. I would stay up late into the night reading his words and fall asleep reciting them like mantras. One night after a workshop in Venice, I fell asleep reciting his poetry and decided to further my connection to him from within a lucid dream.

I became lucid and as soon as I knew that I was dreaming I began calling out, 'Hafiz, come to me! I want to learn from you! Hafiz, come to me! I want to know as you know!'

I walked down a corridor lined with pictures from my life and at the end I saw a man with dark hair and a beard, sitting on a chair. I had no idea what Hafiz looked like, but I just knew it was him.

He looked up at me and then looked towards a cupboard from which the two books I had written fell out onto the floor.

In reply to my plea to 'know as you know', he told me that once I had written as many books as he had and lived as long as he had then I would know as he knew, but for now I had written just two books and would learn so much more as I grew as a man.

As I stood there trying to take in what he had just said, I felt such deep love and guidance coming from him that my heart ached. I felt so held and nurtured by his spirit, and I knew that he represented the best part of me.

I woke up crying and full of an energy that I'd never felt before.

In Your Dreams...

What figures represent aspects of *your* highest potential? What deities, buddhas, angels or ascended masters might they be? Are you ready to invoke them in a lucid dream?

Exercise: Golden Shadow Lucidity

1. Begin by creating a dream plan (*see page 231*) for meeting your golden shadow or a specific golden shadow archetype.

2. Engage your chosen lucid dreaming technique (*see page 221*).

3. In your next lucid dream, engage your dream plan by calling out your statement of intent. For example:

   Golden shadow, come to me! I want to meet my golden shadow!

   or

   Jesus Christ, I want to meet Jesus Christ! *

4. Sometimes your golden shadow will manifest in an obvious way, but sometimes it needs to be discovered, as when I found my older self in the mirror. Whatever manifests, actively embrace the shadow with love. This could be literally by hugging it or by saying to whatever appears:

   I love you. I accept you. I am ready to embrace you!

---

* I called out to meet Jesus Christ in a lucid dream once. It was an amazing experience of incredible light (*see page 237*).

5. In the waking state, try to locate exactly what qualities were represented by whatever may have appeared to you (such as loyalty, love, strength and courage), and then explore how to continue integrating them in your waking life.

These golden qualities are often your unmanifested potential, so see if there are any ways in which you can let them shine even more.

PART III

TRANSMUTING THE SHADOW

'The cave you fear to enter holds the treasure you seek.'

JOSEPH CAMPBELL[1]

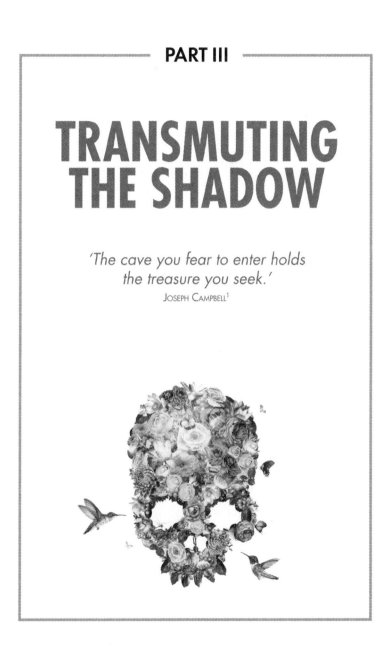

So far we've met and befriended our shadow in both our dreams and our waking life. Now we'll learn how to transmute its energy alchemically through a set of practices that may ask us to rethink our relationship to ourselves in quite extraordinary ways.

We'll explore our ancestral past, our sexual story, our inner demons and our own mortality. These practices may evoke some powerful responses within you, so it is essential that you don't force anything here.

Before embarking on each exercise in this part, I encourage you to pause for a few minutes and ask yourself, 'Is this the right time for me to engage in this process? Do I feel that it's being kind to myself to address this at this time? Do I feel sufficiently confident and supported, both spiritually and/or emotionally, in exploring this part of myself?'

If you feel ready, breathe deeply, open your heart and buckle up. Now is the time to transmute your shadow.

CHAPTER 11

THE ANCESTRAL SHADOW

'What lies behind us and what lies before us are
tiny matters compared to what lies within us.'

Ralph Waldo Emerson[1]

In many ways, our shadow is the product of not only who we are, but also of where we have come from, and so until we acknowledge and accept that, our unhelpful shadow patterns may well keep recurring.

My interest in ancestral shadow work was sparked by a comment from my friend Stephen Victor, who is an esteemed life coach with particular expertise in family constellation work. He said that the ancestral shadow held the key to integrating the personal one and explained why it is so important to integrate it:

If you cut your foot on a large nail, you would rightly take action to heal it. Failing to do so imperils your foot, or life.

Believe it or not, failing to heal ancestral shadow may cost you life and limb too, because so often the root cause of many of our difficulties lies in the energy lines of those who came before us. Freeing ourselves from this conditioning is imperative if we're to live the lives awaiting us.[2]

Of course, this doesn't mean that we should ascribe blame to our ancestral line or reject responsibility for who we are, simply that we should be aware that the ability to respond to our current challenges may be found in our familial past as much as in our present.

And with that in mind, I set out to integrate the energy of my ancestors. I began with my nearest ones: my mum and dad.

In the Shadows of Our Parents

My father once wrote to me: 'The truth is no one tells you how to be a good parent. You rely on human instinct and memories of your own childhood – both good and bad. In my case, having grown up without a father, having sons meant much of the time I was all at sea...'

It took a long time for my dad and me to reach the level of openness and authenticity that those words reveal and the first vital step along the way was when he told me his story...

Steve Biddulph, author of the brilliant *Manhood*, believes that 'without understanding our fathers and knowing them well, we cannot decide what we want to take and what we want to leave of their legacy'[3] and so we inherit their shadow traits by default. He believes that until we come to terms with them, they will haunt us from the inside. Although Biddulph is talking specifically about our father's story, I believe that this can be applied to our mother's story too.

If we can come to know our parents' stories, we can come to better understand why they are the way they are and move our relationship into empathy and understanding, while also starting to become aware of the inherited shadow traits that we may have received and thus enabling ourselves to stop unconsciously playing them out and passing them on to our own children.

Even if one (or both) of your parents was absent, abusive, lost or even dead before you met them, you have a choice: to come to terms with the legacy that they handed to you or to share your life with the ghost of their shadow.

My friend Lama Choyin Rangdrol, a brilliant African-American Buddhist lama, once told me, 'It's important to identify your parents' demons so you can defend yourself from making them your own. Your parents' demons are not your own. With awareness and practice, you can allow yourself to escape their bad habits. Then you are free.'[4]

Exercise: Healing the Parental Shadow

This exercise asks you to spend time alone with your father or mother and to have a series of conversations in which you seek to understand their life, their reasons for being, their successes and their failures. You are encouraged to travel back into their past with them, learn about who they were before they were your parent and learn how they became the person they were when they co-created you.

The aim of this exercise is to humanize your father or mother, to empathize with their role as a person rather than solely as your parent and to compassionately bear witness to their story as a way of helping *them* integrate *their* shadow while you integrate your parental one.

If your father or mother is dead, or you have lost all contact with them, you can still do this exercise either by making a pilgrimage back to their home and significant places in their life and/or through conversations with family members who remember them, using photos if you wish. You could also then write a letter of thanks to them and burn it as a way of ritually sending it to them and of gaining closure over the process.

Step 1

I will outline the complete process below simply as a template of possibility, but I am aware that some parents may be totally unwilling to engage with certain parts of this process, so feel free to do as much or as little of it as possible.

- Ideally, arrange to spend a day with your father or mother, journeying back into their past with them as the tour guide. You don't have to mention shadow integration or anything like that. But let them know that this is not an invitation to argue, that you are not coming armed with old resentments and that your only aim is to hear their story.

- If you can, make a real-life journey back to the place of their birth or where they grew up. Ask them to show you around and to guide you back into their history. If this is too much, simply arrange to go for a long drive or a walk with them, alone and undisturbed.

Step 2

- Once you are alone, start to ask them about the story of their life. Defensiveness may be the 'go to' response from some parents, so take it slowly.

- Below are 10 of the questions that I asked my parents, but of course feel free to change them or to write your own list.

  - *'How was your upbringing?'*

  - *'What was your relationship like with your father and mother?'*

  - *'What were you like as a child?'*

  - *'Do you remember your first kiss?'*

  - *'What was your first job?'*

  - *'Where did you live when you first left home?'*

  - *'What did you dream of doing with your life?'*

  - *'What were you scared of as a child?'*

  - *'How did you feel when you first became a parent?'*

  - *'What was going on in your life when I was born?'*

The answers to these questions led me to ask dozens of others too, but these are a pretty good starting point. They are just suggestions, though, and if your parent is unwilling to answer any, that's totally fine. All you can do is ask.

Step 3

- Within a few days, write them an email or letter of thanks (they will have been waiting), not just for the day you spent together but for anything else you might want to thank them for. Now is the perfect time. You don't have to forget their foibles and you don't even have to have forgiven them for their wrongs yet, but do write to them letting them know that you bear witness to their story and that you are grateful to them for sharing it.

- Don't expect a reply, but if they do reply then feel free to continue the dialogue.

I encourage anybody with a fractured parental relationship to do this exercise. I found it to be a powerful practice that was instrumental in healing the wounded relationship that I had with my father. The evening after we did it, I realized that I'd spent over six hours in uninterrupted conversation with him in what was easily the deepest and longest conversation we'd ever had. Sitting on the train back home, I realized that I'd learned more about my father in those six hours than I had in the previous 30 years. I felt that I now knew some of his story and already I felt greater empathy, greater respect and greater love for him, not just as my father, but as a man.

Healing the Ancestral Shadow

The exploration of our ancestral lineage frees up huge amounts of psychic energy tied up in our family line. We loosen the chains that shackle us to our bloodline and make conscious the ancestral shadow patterns that may have been playing out in the present. Freeing ourselves from these patterns gives us more energy in both our dream and waking lives and allows us to move forward without the burden of so much ancestral conditioning. How can we do it?

Yet again the process is to accept, befriend and embrace the shadow. By tracing back our family line, we can compassionately witness the dark shadows of our ancestors and pay homage to their golden potential by celebrating their success.

Grandmother's Footsteps

I looked out over the cliffs and thought how she would have seen the same sea. Same but different – separated by five generations. I was on the trail of my maternal ancestors, trying to uncover both the dark and golden shadow traits of my familial line as a way to further befriend and integrate my shadow.

I had arrived at the clifftop house on the Isle of Wight, off the south coast of the UK, where my great-great-grandmother once lived, clutching the hand-printed story of my maternal lineage called *When the Women Come*. My aunt had written it as a gift for her boys (my cousins), a gift that would remind them of the long line of fierce female rebels who had created them.

From the house I walked in my great-great-grandmother's footsteps and made the three-mile journey to the tiny 11th-century church where her daughter had played the organ every Sunday. As I walked along the cliffs, I could feel an almost palpable energy that I thought might be from my ancestors. Then, as if to confirm this hunch, I encountered a series of such strange signs and synchronicities within such a small space of time that I struggled to believe them.

They included a street with the same name as my grandmother's street in London (although 100 miles apart), a six-inch Buddha statue embedded into a drystone wall (I still have no idea how to explain that) and finally a Spitfire fighter plane from the same era as my grandfather's time in the army, which flew overhead exactly as I arrived at the church (just in case I hadn't got the message yet).

I was sure of it now – my ancestors knew that I was calling to them and they were calling back to me, using perhaps the only means that past ancestors can use: synchronicity, signs and Spitfire fighter planes.

I continued my research with photo albums, interviews with family members and even a DNA test to trace my genealogy.

Almost the entire family has now become involved in this. A 'Reply All' email that was sent out encouraging us all to share our memories brought us closer than ever before and my auntie became so enthused that she traced the entire family line back to the 1400s. She even instigated a family outing last Christmas to walk in our ancestors' footsteps, at which she made a fire offering to them and raised a toast to their memory! I should add, ours is not usually the kind of family that makes spontaneous fire offerings.

As I reviewed my ancestral line and reflected on the stories of their lives, I saw recurring shadow patterns emerge over and over again: fierce female independence and a strong creative flair* for the golden, and a whole load of secrets, lies and denial for the dark.

Just the process of becoming aware of and witnessing my ancestral shadow traits has changed me. Now, whenever I catch myself about to play out a familial shadow trait (such as secrecy or denial), I pause and remind myself that I have a choice: to continue repeating this pattern or break it for the sake of my future family. This simple change has had profound effects.

---

* I found actors and performers on both sides of my ancestry: a vaudeville music troupe on my mum's and a circus troupe who performed for the Tsar of Russia on my dad's. No wonder I feel so at home on stage.

Exercise: Exploring the Ancestral Shadow

This exercise takes a bit of planning, but it's one that I strongly encourage you to do. Take it slowly and playfully. I advise exploring the happier aspects of your family history first as a way of building a solid foundation of gratitude. This will help support the weight of the heavier aspects that you may uncover.

If you know that there is trauma or abuse in your family's past, feel free to simply acknowledge this when you encounter it, rather than delve too deeply into it. As always, feel free to share your experience with a therapist, coach or trusted friend.

Step 1

- Ideally, arrange to spend a day (or more if you like) with an older family member or close friend of the family who has a good knowledge of your ancestral history.

- Spend the day journeying back into your family's past using photo albums, family artefacts or simply remembered stories to help you to understand who your ancestors were.

   You need not travel back very far if it's not possible. Even just tracing your line back as far as your great-grandmother can be more than enough. This exercise is really about intention and the healing will occur at an energetic level.

Step 2

- If you can, walk in the footsteps of your ancestors and visit their birth places or grave sites. Act like an explorer, seeing, with friendly curiosity, how far back into the past you can go.

Step 3

- Take some time to reflect on both the dark and golden shadows of your family lines. Are there any recurring shadow patterns or themes? Can you see any of these aspects in yourself? If so, then simply bear witness to them with acceptance and send them your love and compassion.

Step 4

- Write a letter to your ancestors in which you acknowledge their stories, send them your love and respectfully state your intention to *release any and all ancestral patterns that no longer serve you.*

- Find a way to 'post' this letter either through ceremonially burning it or perhaps by reading it out loud to yourself in a mirror.

- You might also like to draw a picture of your family line, starting with you and your parents and going back as far as you can remember. Draw a stick person for each family member and then add their names (*see below*).

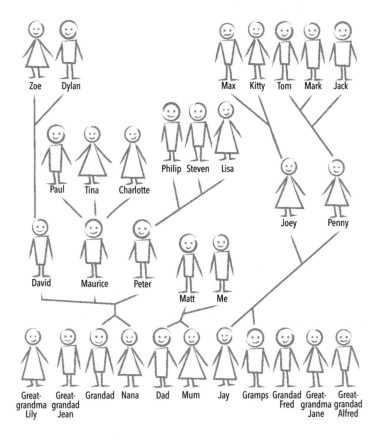

Figure 5: My ancestral line

Wherever we have gathered our shadow material from, whether it is ancestral or self-created, we have to take responsibility for who we are now. We are the only ones who can integrate our ancestral shadow and, more importantly, who can prevent the recurring shadow patterns that we inherited from being passed down the line.

In Your Dreams...

As we trace the energetic line through our ancestry, we can continue our integration through the dreamtime too.

Exercise: Lucidly Embracing Your Ancestors

Meeting your ancestors in a lucid dream can be a deeply healing way to integrate ancestral energy, as lucid dreaming allows for amplified communication with the non-physical realms.

If you are not yet having lucid dreams, you may well find that your ancestors come into your ordinary dreams spontaneously, as a side-effect of doing the exercise above, but if not, then try setting your intention to meet and to show love to your ancestors in your next dream by reciting over and over as you drift into the hypnagogic state:

Tonight in my dreams I connect with my ancestors.
I call my ancestors into my dreams!

To try ancestral integration through lucid dreaming, once lucid, if you feel that you are playing out unhelpful ancestral patterns, you could call out:

With love and respect, I release my unhelpful ancestral patterns!

Or for a more general befriending and healing request, once lucid you could call out:

I want to meet my ancestors! Ancestors, come to me!

or

Ancestors, I love you! I heal and reconcile my ancestral line!

Then lovingly embrace or even have a dialogue with whoever appears.

When I first tried this technique in a lucid dream, I called out: 'Ancestors, I love you! I send love to my ancestors!' In response to this a mirror appeared. When I looked in it, I saw myself in the form of my grandmother. After the initial shock, I was moved to tears as I realized what the dream was telling me: every time we look at ourselves in the mirror, we see our ancestors looking back at us. They are always with us. They live in our reflection. (*To read that dream in full, see page 235.*)

1. Begin by creating a dream plan (*see page 231*) for meeting your ancestors.

2. Engage your chosen lucid dreaming techniques (*see page 221*).

3. In your next lucid dream, engage your dream plan by calling out your statement of intent to the dream, for example, 'Ancestors, come to me!'

    Be open to any new dream characters or changes in the dream that occur. Your internal ancestors may appear in personified or more subtle form, so stay aware.

    Whatever happens, actively embrace the ancestral manifestation with love, either by literally hugging it (this would be the ideal) or by sending the dreamscape your love through affirming:

    I love you, my ancestors. I integrate your energy.

CHAPTER 12

EXPLORING THE SEXUAL SHADOW

'Much of our sexuality is shrouded in the shadow. Understanding and accepting our unique sexual mosaic with compassionate light is a necessary step in our growth.'

Keith Witt[1]

Nowadays, at an outer level we see sex and sexualized images every time we look at an advertising billboard or switch on the TV, and yet at an inner level there is an underlying and almost universally experienced suppression of our sexuality. Suppression creates shadow, and when this is combined with the fear and shame that are so often tied up in our personal relationship with sex, it comes as no surprise that our shadow will almost always have sexual content. For many of us, sexual experiences and the projection of sexual dogmas onto us by early-life authority figures will have created some of our densest shadow content.

One of the best ways of transmuting the energy of our sexual shadow is of course to shine the light of awareness into its depths.

Masks in the Mirror

Apart from Tibetan Buddhism, the spiritual lineage I've had the most personal experience of is the ancient Toltec Mexihca tradition of Mexico. For the past three years I have co-facilitated workshops on lucid dreaming, and more recently conscious dying, with my friend Sergio Magaña. Sergio is the author of *The Toltec Secret* and *Caves of Power*, and in 2013 he was named the Club UNESCO representative for the preservation of the Toltec Mexihca tradition.

In this tradition it is believed that in order to integrate the shadow we first need to accept that we have these aspects within us and then be prepared to face them through practices that ask us to look directly into our shadow side.

Some of the shamanic practices that I've learned from Sergio involve ingesting the powdered body of a snake in order to invite the spirit of the serpent into dreams, as well as breathwork techniques and ritual dances that align the subtle energy centres. But one of the most powerful and effective shadow practices that I've been taught by him involves masks, mirrors and dis-identification with our personal story around sex and sexuality.

How Does It Work?

The set-up of this exercise can seem rather bizarre, but stay with me, because once you see how it works, it will make more sense.

Essentially, you stand in front of a mirror, wearing a mask, and talk out loud for 36 minutes about your relationship to sex and sexuality. You do this for at least nine days straight. The aim is to download the entire story of your sexuality and all the shadow content that it contains from the darkness of your unconscious into the light of your awareness.

The idea behind this is that your sense of self-identification is strongly linked to your face. Think about it. When you imagine a person, it's their face that you see in your mind's eye, isn't it?

So, your face is synonymous with your ego-identity and so by hearing your sexual story told by another face (that of the mask) your story and your ego-identity start to become separated.* At a subliminal level, your mind starts to dis-identify with the story being told and with all the co-authors of that story (partners, lovers, parents and friends), who added to its narrative. This dis-identification can dissolve habits, traumas and energetic blocks pertaining to your sexuality in a very powerful way.

Sergio suggests that you 'talk about the social, religious and scientific paradigms that you have been exposed to and how they've affected your sexuality. The mask will help you to stop identifying with your sexual story and be free of this conditioning. You will also release your trapped sexual energy, the most powerful energy you have, and harness this energy for your dream work and spiritual practice.'[2]

My Journey into the Mirror

As a sceptical Buddhist, and a sceptical British Buddhist at that, this whole mask/mirror/sex thing just seemed a bit too 'woo-woo' for me. I just couldn't imagine how talking about my sexual history in front of a mirror while wearing a mask could have any psychological benefit at all.

Eventually I gave it a shot, though. For the first five minutes of the first session I really thought I was wasting my time and I felt genuinely embarrassed to be offloading my sexual baggage in front of a bathroom mirror while wearing an ill-fitting *Lion King* mask.

---

* The crux of this technique comes from wearing the mask. If you did this exercise plain-faced, you would simply further concretize the connection between your identity and your sexual story.

But soon interesting things started to happen. In one session, my reflection start to change and the image of the mask became almost animated. Then, in another session, as I spoke, my sexual story actually began to sound like someone else's. It was strange, but it was almost as if I was hearing my voice talking about a stranger's sexual problems. I could feel myself starting to dis-identify with the story. So much of it had happened so long ago. Why was I still judging myself for stuff I'd done as a teenager?

Soon I found myself talking about sexual shame that I hadn't recalled in over 20 years and by the end of the practice I was having quite profound insights into my relationship with sexuality.

I saw how my sexual story had started early on in life. I remembered the first time I'd seen porn and how I felt scared by it, the time I felt sexually attracted to another boy, the long conversations with my mum about how menstruation worked and the little girl I fell in love with at the video-games arcade when I was eight years old.

So many memories had been buried, unconsciously weighing me down, shackling me to a myth of who I thought I was. I felt so much lighter afterwards, more authentic and more aware of how my sexual story was a myth shaped by circumstance, shame and a longing for love.

Lovability/Sex-ability

One of the deepest insights I had while doing the masks exercise came through tracing back a long-standing sexual complex (the belief that I had to be a 'good' lover in order to be lovable) to my first kiss at the age of 10. My friend and I were playing spin the bottle with a group of older girls and as I was experiencing my first kiss everybody laughed at me as I struggled to work out the dynamics of kissing and ended up making embarrassing slurping noises.

I hadn't spoken of that incident for years. And yet I realized that afterwards, 10-year-old Charlie had made some sort of unconscious pledge to be 'good' at sexual stuff so that the pain of that humiliation never happened again. In so doing, I had created a deep shadow complex around sexuality and self-worth.

There were other instances in my teens and twenties that served to concretize this complex, but essentially I'd been holding the unconscious belief that my lovability was dependent on my sexual ability ever since that first kiss. Simply tracing the origin of this complex, naming it 'lovability/sex-ability' and then witnessing it with acceptance released the stranglehold that it had over me. Remembering that single buried memory changed my life.

Owning our sexual story can be hard, but not nearly as hard as trying to keep it hidden. So I strongly encourage anyone who has heavy shadow energy in their sexual story to try this exercise.

Exercise: Sexual Shadow Mask Work

The full version of this practice is called 'The Venerable Old Man' and requires that you do the entire practice in one marathon session of 12 hours straight! You can take breaks, eat and have short naps, but essentially you recapitulate your entire sexual history in one epic 12-hour session. I have done this full version and it was without doubt one of the most powerful spiritual practices I have ever done. I integrated more of my sexual baggage in those 12 hours than in the previous 12 years. (For a full description of it, see Sergio Magaña's *The Toltec Secret*.)

The version below is a specially adapted one that Sergio has said can be done by those not yet ready to do the full 12-hour version. All that it requires is 36 minutes in front of the mirror for at least nine days straight. I have done this day-by-day version too and it's still very powerful.

Step 1

- Buy or find yourself at least three different masks. They can be any type you like, but those that cover your full face may be better. Ones from a toy shop will be fine, but if you want to use more fancy ones then go for it. When I did it, I chose particularly ridiculous farm animal ones to help bring humour to the process.

Step 2

You can do this at any time of day or night, but doing it before bed allows you to weave the thread of integration directly into your dreams too.

- Set an alarm for 36 minutes later*, put on one of the masks and then stand or sit in front of a mirror.

- Look into the mirror and talk, out loud and in the first person, about all there is to know about your relationship to sex and sexuality.

  Talk about absolutely everything: porn, taboos, perversions, sexual orientation and your entire sexual history from every angle you can imagine. Talk about everything you know, everything you have been taught, been programmed to believe and truly believe about sex and sexuality. Explore your fears and fantasies. Be totally uncensored – nothing is off-limits. Say the unsayable and offer any and all sexual shame to the mirror. Essentially, whatever you would say to a sexologist or psychotherapist is what you say to the reflection in the mirror.

- When the alarm sounds after 36 minutes, step away from the mirror and remove the mask.

Step 3

- Repeat Step 2 for at least nine days straight. If you miss a day, you should start again if possible. You can do it at different times each day, but make sure that you have done one session per 24 hours.

---

* You might be thinking, *Why the big deal over the number 36?* In the ancient Mexihca tradition each 24-hour cycle is broken up into 11 fractions of the day and 9 of the night. This led to 9 becoming the number of the night, darkness and the shadow. This number is then multiplied by four (a number significant because of the four elements and the four Moon phases) to get the special number 36.

Change masks whenever you like, but be sure not to change your mask while looking in the mirror, for the illusion may be broken.

- If you feel you need more than nine days, then keep going for 36 minutes every day until you feel that there is nothing more to be said.

- Some tips:

    - *You can choose certain relationships or aspects of your sexuality and spend a whole 36-minute session on each one, or you can just be spontaneous.*

    - *Offer up all of your emotional and sexual baggage to the mirror. Tears and laughter are part of the process.*

    - *Allow yourself to really experience the emotional energy of past events, because feeling the feeling leads to healing.*

    - *Be creative. Thirty-six minutes can seem like quite a long time to be talking uninterrupted, so periods of silence, just watching the reflection, are fine too.*

    - *If any distressing memories surface that you feel require professional help, don't hesitate to seek the advice of a therapist or trained professional.*

Step 4

- Although not found in the Toltec tradition, an additional step that I found particularly beneficial was, when the mask and mirror work was finished, to create a simple stick man drawing of my sexual history (a bit like a family tree of sexual partners) and then ceremonially burn it while stating:

I release any and all non-beneficial energetic
ties to every person pictured here.

An ex-armed forces officer called Gareth found this exercise to be particularly powerful. After he completed it, he emailed me saying, 'Woah … that was hard core! The first chunk was difficult to look at: father, mother, sexual role models, porn, gender, self-esteem … but soon I saw how fluid sexuality is and how sexual energy underpins so much more than what we class as "erotic". It was a very deep exercise for me and incredibly liberating.'

In Your Dreams...

Be extra attentive to your dreams while you are doing the mask work, because you may find, especially if you do this exercise before bed, that your dreams are affected by whatever you have been telling the mirror.

This is because when you free up and dis-identify with your emotional patterns, your dreams, which are dictated by these patterns to a large degree, will naturally start to change. As you download the memories that you relate to the mirror, you free up space in your unconscious mind, allowing lucid dreaming and dreams of insight to manifest more readily.

The Red Dream

There is another practice from the Toltec Mexihca tradition that allows a dreamer to heal trauma, sexual or otherwise, in a very powerful way.

As a foetus in the womb, the first light that we see is red. This is because it filters through our mother's skin. It is often referred to as 'the red fog of creation' or 'the red light of the cosmic dream'. In the Toltec Mexihca tradition it is believed that in the womb we are dreaming of the person we were and the person we will be, and we're doing it at the moment when our physical body is being created and the light around us is red. Therefore, if we're able to turn everything in our dreams red, our body receives the message that this is a dream of new creation and so can heal itself (and the mind that drives it) in remarkable ways.

A 'red dream' is defined as a dream in which everything is red. It is very rare to have such a dream spontaneously,* but we can invoke one once we are lucid.

---

* If we have a non-lucid red dream, we'll only know about it the next morning when we're recalling our dreams. Even though we weren't lucid, the healing energy of the 'red fog of creation' may still have a beneficial effect.

Whether spontaneous or lucidly created, once we are in a red dream, we can call out for healing or for anything that we want to create in our life. My first experience of a red dream came a couple of years ago.

> I was dreaming that I was in a room that had a huge red carpet in it. Then I saw that the drapes on the walls were red too, and the light fixtures, and even the chairs. It was so strange to see all these red things that I became aware that I was dreaming and instantly thought, Hang on, this looks like a red dream. It is a red dream!

> I knew that a red dream was a dream of creation in which we could transform our deepest emotional patterns and so I called out, still fully lucid, 'I am healed of any and all sexual traumas! I am healed of any and all sexual traumas!'

> After I had yelled that out, a huge lorry full of very friendly people and a sound system pulled up, and the dream became a huge dance party. It was as if the whole dream was celebrating the healing of the red dream.

Whatever you want to create in your life, be it freedom from sexual trauma, integration of a shadow aspect or healing of an ailment, a red dream can facilitate this in a very powerful way.

Exercise: The Sacred Place of Red Dreams

1. The most direct way to have a red dream is to become lucid and turn the dream red. You may find that it is the redness in the dream that makes you become lucid (as happened with me), but if not then, once lucid, call out for everything to become red and use the power of your intent to make everything turn red.

2. Call out for your particular healing, for example:

I am healed of my sexual shame
or
I integrate the shadow of my sexuality.

Non-lucid Integration

Even if we learn to have lucid dreams every night of our life, still 95 per cent of our dream experience will be non-lucid, simply based on the multitude of dreams we have each night.* This means that although lucid dreams can be brilliantly direct ways to effect deep change from within, the vast majority of our psychological integration happens during non-lucid dreaming.

In fact, some of the most powerful dreams I've ever had have not been lucid ones. It's almost as if the messages from these dreams was so big that they simply wanted me to witness them, rather than direct them.

Let's look at an example of this kind of powerful non-lucid integration.

An artist named Tazeem was particularly interested in exploring her sexual shadow. To further her integration, she decided to take part in a sexual Tantra seminar. The night after the seminar, she had a dream in which she integrated deep-seated feelings of sexual and bodily shame that she had carried ever since she was a child growing up in an Asian-Muslim home of extreme sexual suppression. She told me:

In my dream I am bleeding heavily on my period. Several pairs
of my knickers stained with dried blood are lying scattered
on the floor of my home. I feel ashamed that my soiled

---

* Based on an average eight-hour sleep cycle, most people will have four to five dream periods each night. Each dream period might consist of one or many dreams.

underwear is lying around and I try to kick them out of sight of my friend who is with me.

Then an unknown man enters. He bends down and in a knowing way he picks up a pair of my bloodstained knickers. He slowly unfolds them and holds them up. There in the middle, where the blood should be, is the most exquisite painting of a bird's wing. The pattern is so delicate and the detail so intricate – an arrangement of black and white feathers with a flash of gold too. The beauty of it stuns me.

Suddenly the room is full of people who are also looking in awe at the beauty of what my bloodstained knickers have become.

Then I look around the room and see that it has transformed into an art gallery space, but with bare walls.

A second man bends down and picks up another pair of my knickers and opens them with reverence, and this time in place of bloodstains there is a butterfly, again painted in amazing detail. Everyone gasps in wonder as they see it.

Finally, they all start picking up the knickers and hanging them on the walls like works of art. The bloodstained knickers have become treasured artworks in a public gallery and people are admiring their beauty.

Tazeem's dream showed that, due to her willingness to explore her sexual shadow, the source of her shame had become a source of beauty.

When I asked her how she felt after the dream, she said, 'When I woke, I felt excited. For decades my dreams were full of sexual shame, humiliation and rejection. They have been evolving slowly in the years that I have been doing dream work and shadow work, but this dream made me feel as though I had seen a miracle.'

CHAPTER 13

THE PEACOCK AND THE POISON

*'Go to places that scare you in order to
discover the Buddha within yourself.'*

Machig Labdrön[1]

A unique aspect of Tibetan Buddhism is that it encourages the integration of any and all aspects of the mind, dark and light. There is a great image that is used to describe this approach: the peacock that eats the poison.

In Indian folklore, the source of the peacock's rainbow plumage is believed to be the poisonous plants that it eats. It's the alchemical transmutation of the poison that is believed to give the plumage its beauty.

Most people are not like peacocks, however. Most avoid their internal poisonous plants. This seems logical, but unfortunately it means that the plants are still there and still growing.

Some people like to acquire knowledge about the poisonous plants and find antidotes for them or methods of uprooting them. This is okay but it still sees the plants as a negative force and misses the opportunity to transmute the poison into the power of awakening.

It is said that the Tibetan Buddhist practitioner must be like the peacock: one who can 'transform the poisons of ignorance, attachment and aversion into the medicine of wisdom and compassion'.[2] This approach, of literally digesting and gaining nourishment from the shadow, will allow us to utilize potentially poisonous emotions as food for the feast of spiritual growth and enlightenment.

Tibetan Buddhism is well known for its Tantric practices. These are based on the Tantras, a series of teachings given by the Buddha, which explore the transformation of the mind using profound meditation techniques.* Tantra is all about transformation.

In Tibetan Buddhism, all that we are, both helpful and harmful, is seen as the material of transformation. Buddhist scholar Rob Preece believes that practitioners must get to know their shadow side, because when they do the Tantric meditations they will almost certainly come face to face with it.

He told me, 'We need to recognize what is buried and unconscious, so that it can be released from the dark and transformed. It requires great courage and great honesty to do this, but it is essential.'[3]

The Ogress of the Rock

Although it's important to stress that Tibetan Buddhism does not include the term 'the shadow',† it takes a wholly Tantric approach to the dark side and is full of stories of practitioners integrating their shadows on the path to awakening.

There was once a yogi who was experiencing trouble from a dark force while he was meditating in his cave on the side of

---

* One of those meditation techniques is sexual, which is perhaps why people so often think of 'Tantric sex' when they hear the term 'Tantric'. However, in Tibetan Buddhist Tantra, the transformation of sexual energy is just one of hundreds of transformational practices and so the term 'Tantric' generally does not refer to anything sexual.

† At an ultimate level, the very ideas of dark, light and shadow are redundant in the non-dualistic Buddhist view of reality.

a cliff. He explained to his teacher that each night when he slept, a huge ogress would climb up the cliff, enter his cave and try to devour him. But he had the situation under control: that night when the monster entered his cave, he would stab her with his knife.

His teacher had a different plan, though. Instead of stabbing the monster, he asked the yogi to take a piece of chalk and draw a white cross on her stomach.

The yogi was surprised by this plan, but trusted his teacher and so that night he slept with the piece of chalk in his hand.

As expected, the ogress climbed up the cliff and into the yogi's cave, whereupon he jumped to his feet and with two slashes of the chalk made a white cross on her stomach. She immediately vanished and he fell back to sleep.

The next morning the yogi woke up and looked down to find a white chalk cross on his stomach. And with that, the ogress of his dark side was integrated.

Embracing the Darkness

To explore this approach to the dark side in more depth, I met up with my friend Ian Baker, an acclaimed Buddhist author who has co-written books with HH the Dalai Lama.

As he guided me around an art exhibition that he had curated, called 'Tibet's Secret Temple', he told me, 'Tantric Buddhism consists of making the darkness conscious. It's all about reorienting how we look at things. Rather than a form of spiritual bypassing in which we just move towards the light, Tantra is about embracing the totality – which absolutely means going deeply into the darkness, into all that isn't yet conscious. From the point of view of Tantra, everything that can be embraced *should be* embraced; otherwise we live only partial lives.'[4]

The whole idea of Tantric Buddhism is about a radical and compassionate embrace of all phenomena. As the great 11th-century female master Machig Labdrön once said, 'In order to realize the essence of consciousness you must approach what you find repulsive and go to places that scare you in order to discover the Buddha within.'[5]

Ian went on to explain how Tantric Buddhism is not about rejecting experience, but about moving into it more deeply and using even things that we might classify as frightening or dangerous as opportunities to enlarge our relationship to reality as a whole.

Although we often think of Buddhism as the middle path between extremes, Tantric Buddhism is different – it's actually about integrating extremes. It's about pushing the body and mind beyond their habitual limits as a way of being able to encompass, with compassion, a larger experience of reality. But of course, this is why Tantra is sometimes referred to as 'licking honey from a razor's edge', because although it offers the sweetness of the blissful experience, if you lick the honey incorrectly, you can hurt yourself and others.

The most important thing Ian said, though, was: 'Compassion is always the key motivation underlying all these practices. They are not done for ego aggrandizement, but to achieve a state of inseparability and altruistic empathy for all beings.'

As you see, although the terminology of 'shadow integration' is not used as such, the path of Tantric Buddhism is imbued with it.

Golden Buddhas

It's not just the dark shadow that the Tantric Buddhist path seeks to integrate, but the golden shadow too. In fact, as we learned earlier, the recognition of our Buddha nature, our divine potential, forms the basis of the entire path.

As well as this, I believe that the Tibetan teachings make particularly skilful use of our propensity to project our golden shadow outwards through its focus on the relationship between spiritual teacher and disciple. As a Tibetan Buddhist practitioner in a formal 'student–teacher' relationship, I am particularly interested in how 'guru* devotion' may harness golden shadow projection to help reveal our own capacity for enlightenment.

My theory is this: the wisdom of our inner teacher, who is the ultimate teacher of course, is so awesome that it can often only be seen through proxy, via projection onto an outer teacher. This outer teacher serves as a template for awakening upon which the student projects their own Buddha nature. Through this process the golden shadow potential of the student becomes not only easier to recognize but often magnified by it. The real crux of the process, though, is found in what the teacher does next.

An authentic teacher will be aware that ultimately the enlightened qualities that the student has projected onto them have to be returned and so rather than soaking up this devotional projection, they reflect it back at them.

The primary duty of the teacher is to bring the disciple into an awareness of their own enlightened nature by handing them back their projections. If done correctly, this can be an incredibly skilful means of awakening the dormant qualities of enlightenment that lie within the student.

It is only because Lama Yeshe Rinpoche, my Buddhist master, has integrated his own shadow to such a high degree that the

---

*   Interestingly the Sanskrit term *guru* comes from the same root as the word for 'heavy' or 'weighty', for it is a person who has the solidity and condensed power of spiritual awareness. A person who has fully integrated their shadow becomes more substantial as they step into the power that comes from having illuminated the darkness.

process described above becomes possible. In my mind, he is undoubtedly an awakened being, and in his wakefulness I'm almost certain that one of the many ways he is working with his students is through reflecting their own golden shadow projections back at them.

However, if the teacher has yet to fully integrate their own shadow, this kind of 'devotional projection' can lead to terrible abuse, the cost of which may harm the teacher as much as the student. Rather than reflecting the golden shadow projection back to the student, the inauthentic teacher may soak up the projection. This leads at best to the ego aggrandizement of the teacher and the disempowerment of the student and at worst to the abuse scandals that have become synonymous with so many 'guru' figures.

So, is it really worth the risk? If the teacher is authentic, then yes, I believe it is, as it can greatly accelerate your spiritual progress. But I would advise you to spend a lot of time researching, investigating and examining a spiritual teacher before you become their disciple. If you want to get to the mountaintop, you need to be sure that your guide not only knows the way, but has spent enough time up there to be able to guide you there too. They need to know where the dangerous crevasses are, which ropes to use in which conditions and how to predict possible dangers on the path. Just as you would check the credentials of a guide taking you up Everest, check those of your spiritual teacher. The stakes are just as high.

Tonglen

Tonglen is a Tibetan term that means 'giving and taking' and it's not only a powerful shadow integration technique, it's also a brilliant example of how the seemingly paradoxical approach of the peacock and the poison is used to transform everything we usually avoid into the plumage of awakening. It can be used to heal past relationships, soften hardened hearts and transform our shadow into the energy of enlightenment.

As my first Buddhist teacher, Sogyal Rinpoche, said, 'Of all the practices I know, the practice of *tonglen* is one of the most useful and the most powerful.'[6] He explained that it destroyed hard-heartedness and egocentricity while unlocking our natural capacity for love.

Quite simply, it asks us to imagine sending all our love and joy to others in the form of white light, while imagining relieving them of their pain and suffering by inhaling it in the form of black smoke.

Some people may understandably feel worried about breathing in the suffering of others, worried that it is something that might be toxic or unsafe. In fact, the power of the compassion generated by *tonglen* protects us completely. As we imagine taking in the suffering of another person, it not only heals them, but it also heals *us*, through the infinite healing power that we invoke through doing so. It may seem paradoxical (as the Tantric approach often does), but it is totally safe and has very powerful effects.

When I first did *tonglen*, I was 19 and did it for the girl who had broken my heart. After the session, I switched on my cell phone and she had text messaged me for the first time in weeks, saying, 'Are you doing a meditation thing? It feels like you're haunting me, but in a nice way.'

More recently a lady in one of my workshops did it for her son, and when she switched her phone on in the break, he had messaged her, saying, 'Mum, are you doing your voodoo stuff again? Feels like you are, anyway.'

This practice works. It shifts something. It moves energy. It heals both the sender and receiver. Let's practise it now.

Exercise: *Tonglen* Meditation

To begin with, we will offer *tonglen* to a loved one to whom we wish to send healing.

Step 1

- Allocate a certain length of time for this exercise (anything from five minutes to 20 minutes, but I suggest five minute to start with).

- Sit on a chair or cushion.

- Take a moment to come into an awareness of your breath. Just notice when you are breathing in and notice when you are breathing out.

- Notice three inhalations and exhalations before you begin.

- With your eyes open or closed, imagine a loved one sitting before you.

- Remind yourself that all beings have Buddha nature and that it is the power of your Buddha nature that you are harnessing during this practice.

Step 2

- Next, think of the ways in which this loved one may have suffered. Reflect on the fact that they will have experienced heartbreak, illness or suffering, just as you have, and resolve to relieve their suffering.

- Now, with the energy of that loving resolve, imagine that as you inhale, you breathe in all the pain and suffering of this person in the form of dark smoke.

- Imagine that as the smoke leaves the person, they are relieved of their pain and suffering.

- Imagine that the dark smoke leaves their body, enters into you through your nostrils and goes down into your heart, where it is transformed by the power of your compassion and dissolves into white light.

Step 3

- Then, as you breathe out, imagine that you are breathing out all your joy, happiness and love to the person in the form of healing white light.

- Imagine that as this white light of love flows from you to them that they are completely filled with love and happiness.

Step 4
- Repeat the three-step process of taking in their suffering in the form of dark smoke as you inhale, transforming it in your heart area and then sending them all your love in the form of pure white light as you exhale. Spend at least a few minutes doing this.

Step 5
This step is not always included, but recommended by the Tibetan lama Akong Rinpoche, especially when working with a person who is sick or dying.

- As you approach the end of your allocated time for the exercise, imagine that the dark smoke becomes gradually thinner and paler as the suffering is slowly removed until what you breathe in is the same white light that you breathe out. Healing white light flows from the person into you and from you into them. You are both now sending and receiving healing white light.

Step 6
- After some time, allow the visualization to fade and your breath to return to its natural rhythm.

- Take a moment to dedicate the beneficial energy of this exercise to yourself and all living beings.

Exercise: *Tonglen* for Our Shadow

The most revolutionary thing you can do is to send your enemies your love. To do so is to transform the very foundation of the shadow.

So I encourage you to do *tonglen* for any person you perceive has wronged you, anyone you blame, anyone you fear, anyone who has caused you pain or brought shame upon you, anyone you still bear a grudge against or who still bears a grudge against you.

The energy of these people will hold power in your shadow. As long as you hold on to what they did to you, you continue to uphold the blame, shame, fear and pain that creates the shadow.

Naturally you may find taking in the suffering of a person whom you hold a grudge against more difficult than doing it for a loved one, so take it slowly, be gentle with yourself and know that even to consider sending love to those who have wronged us is a huge step towards integration.

- Follow exactly the same steps as above, but this time imagine someone or something that particularly triggers your shadow, or even a symbolic representation of a dark shadow trait such as anger or fear of failure, for example.

- There are no limits to this practice. You can even do it to yourself. Simply offer *tonglen* to any aspect of yourself, other people or the world that you are currently unwilling to love.

In Your Dreams...

Before we move on, I should add that there is a way to add even more power to the practice of *tonglen*: by doing it within a lucid dream.

Once you become lucid in your dream, you can practise *tonglen* on a dream character or any shadow aspect that might be present in the dream. As you might expect, this has a very powerful effect on the mind.

I once met a shadow aspect in a lucid dream who told me, as I approached him for a hug, 'I am your repressed capacity for violence. You will never defeat me!' I was quite taken aback upon hearing that, but still tried to embrace him. He didn't much like being hugged, though, so I wrestled him to the floor and practised *tonglen* on him. I inhaled his anger and violence in the form of black smoke while sending him my love. He eventually shrank and then disappeared into light.

Dining with Demons

In Tibetan Buddhism the term 'demon' does not refer to an evil entity, but simply anything within us that prevents us from recognizing our Buddha nature.

Machig Labdrön was once asked by her son to define a demon. She replied, 'That which is called a demon is not some great black thing that petrifies whoever sees it. A demon is anything that obstructs the achievement of freedom.'[7]

Some of the most prevalent demons are said to be those of disturbing emotions: greed, anger and hatred. There's also the demon of procrastination, laziness and the failure to engage our spiritual practice.

The greatest demon of all, though, is the demon of our judgemental dualistic thinking. (That's a demon that I can really relate to.) This demon, created from the illusory ego, is the most insidious demon there is, and one that has possessed us all to some degree. It's said that to train our mind out of this mode of egocentricity is to transform all our demons at once.

In Buddhism all of our so-called demons are sourced from our own mind and are often simply aspects of our unintegrated shadow. As the Tibetan saint Milarepa said, 'Take a demon as a demon and it'll harm you; know a demon is in your mind and you'll be free of it... Once one understands that, even your demons will become deities. I fear no demons: I welcome them!'[8]

But how does one transform the common human demons of egocentricity, anger and fear into the divine beings of awakening? Through courage, love and acceptance: the core elements of a profound practice called 'Feeding Your Demons'.

Demons into Deities

There is a woman alive today who is thought to be an emanation of the female master of demons, Machig Labdrön. She has carried the torch of 'demon transformation' from the 11th century into the 21st. Her name is Lama Tsultrim Allione and she has created a practice called 'Feeding Your Demons,'* which is explored in a book of the same name. It is an imagination exercise in which you personify, befriend and feed your personal demons as a way of transforming them into allies, divine aspects of yourself.

Lama Tsultrim defines a demon as 'anything that's taking your energy'. For her, demons are based on ego-clinging, and they manifest as things like our addictions, our fears, grief, depression, anxiety, paranoia, health issues and pain. She believes that our fears, obsessions and addictions are all parts of ourselves that have become 'demonic' by being split off, disowned and battled against.

She says, 'When you try to flee from your demons, they pursue you... But to feed and then transform them is to achieve true freedom!'[9]

The practice asks you to choose a demon that you wish to transform. It could be the demon of an old habit, a fear or phobia, self-doubt or a lack of confidence.

You then imagine this demon personified, sitting in front of you, and after befriending it through empathic dialogue, you dissolve your body into liquid light and feed yourself to it. This feeding doesn't make the demon bigger or stronger, though, it actually placates it and allows you to request that it transforms into an ally, a representation of benevolent power.

---

* The practice is inspired by the highly esoteric practice of Chöd (meaning 'to cut through'), which was created by Machig Labdrön.

You then receive certain commitments from this benevolent ally before it dissolves itself into healing light, which enters into you.

Finally, you dissolve yourself into light and become one with everything.

Sounds pretty intense, doesn't it? It is, but it's also totally safe and an incredibly beneficial way to integrate your inner demons and transform them into light. In fact, when I asked Lama Tsultrim whether the practice was suitable for everyone, this is what she said:

> Yes. I wrote Feeding Your Demons *specifically for a mainstream audience. You don't have to be Buddhist to practise it either. It is definitely beneficial for everyone.'*
>
> *The practice helps to articulate the shadow aspect of the psyche in a very specific way. The usual approach to demons is to ignore them, to fight them or to get rid of them in some other way. Nurturing demons might seem dangerous, because we are afraid that they will take over.*
>
> *However, repression builds up to an explosion and demons get stronger with the battle as we put our energy into them. If we feed our demons, it actually releases this repressed tension and transforms a demon into an ally.[10]*

The following exercise takes you through the five-step practice, as taught by Lama Tsultrim Allione.

Exercise: Feeding Your Demons

Nine Relaxation Breaths

Take nine deep relaxation breaths with long exhalations: for the first three breaths, breathe in and bring the breath to any tension in the body, releasing it with the exhalation. For the second three breaths, inhale into any emotional tension, feel where you hold it in your body and release it with the exhalation. And lastly, breathe into any mental tension. Feel where you hold nervousness, worries or mental blockages in your body and release them with the exhalation.

Motivation

Generate a heartfelt motivation to practice for the benefit of one's self and all beings.

Step 1: Find the Demon

- Think about the demon you are working with today. The demon of an old habit? The demon of a fear or phobia? The demon of self-doubt? The demon of lack of confidence? The demon of a past trauma? Decide which demon to work with.

- What is the location of the demon in your body?

- What is the shape/colour/texture/temperature of the demon in your body?

Step 2: Personify the Demon and Ask It What It Needs.

- Now allow this energy to move out of your body and become personified in front of you. Visualize the demon in front of you.

- What does it look like? (Size, colour, gender? What is its character like?)

- Now you are going to ask the demon some questions.

  - *Ask the demon what it wants: 'What is it that you want from me?'*

  - *Ask the demon what it needs: 'What need do you have that is behind what you want?'*

  - *Ask the demon how it would feel if it gets what it needs: 'If you get what you need, how will you feel?'*

Step 3: Become the Demon

- Now, immediately change places with the demon (so that you are facing the chair or cushion you were seated on) and enter the demon's body. Become the demon. Allow yourself a little time to 'sit in its shoes'.

- How does it feel to be in the demon's body? How does your normal self look from the demon's point of view?

- Now answer these three questions from the point of view of the demon:

  - *What I want from you is...*

  - *What I need from you is...*

  - *What I would feel if I get what I need is...*

Step 4: Feed the Demon and Meet the Ally

- Now come back to your original place, enter back into your own body and see the demon still there in front of you.

- Remember how the demon will feel when it gets what it really needs? With this feeling in your body, dissolve your body into nectar and vizualize the nectar entering the demon. Maybe the demon eats the nectar of your body? Maybe the demon inhales the nectar? Maybe the nectar flows into its body like rays of light?

- See the demon being nourished by the nectar that you are feeding it; the nectar of your own body.

- Keep feeding the demon until it is totally satisfied. If the demon seems insatiable, imagine how it would look if it were completely satisfied. Keep feeding it, and now imagine that your demon is totally satisfied.

Meeting the Ally

- Now that your demon is totally satisfied we ask an ally to appear in its place. Invite an ally to appear in place of the demon on the chair in front of you, and visualize the ally appearing.

- What does the ally look like? Size/colour/gender/ character?

- Now ask these questions to the ally:

  - *How will you help me?*

  - *How will you protect me?*

  - *What pledge do you make to me?*

- Now change places with the ally and enter its body. Become the ally, and answer the following questions from the point of view of the ally:

  - *I will help you by…*

  - *I will protect you by…*

  - *I pledge I will…*

Return to your original position, facing the ally.

- Imagine that the ally dissolves into light in front of you. Feel the energy of help and protection coming from the ally into you; feel its energy entering every cell of your body.

- Now imagine that you dissolve into light too.

Step 5: Rest in Awareness

- Rest in the state that is present when the ally dissolves into you and you dissolve into emptiness. Let your mind relax; just rest in awareness.

- Now open your eyes and, as you do so, recall the feeling you had when the ally's energy dissolved into your body.

- Dedicate the beneficial energy of the practice to all beings.

To explore this practice further I encourage you to read the book *Feeding Your Demons* or, to be guided through the practice by Lama Tsultrim herself, visit www.taramandala.org to check her teaching schedule.

In Your Dreams...

The following practice asks you to invoke one of your personal demons in the lucid dream state. The inspiration for the technique came from a young man named Maxwell. He had experienced hearing voices for many years. There was one voice in particular, the most aggressive one, which he had often dreamed of getting rid of. This voice was called Darren.

In a lucid dream Maxwell called out for Darren and a personification of him appeared. Maxwell told me:

> *When I saw him in the lucid dream, I just threw my arms around him and hugged him. I was actually hugging one of the voices in my head — someone I'd always considered to be an enemy, a threat. It felt so good to hug him, and he returned the hug and held me.*
>
> *Then I asked him, 'Why are you here? Why are you in my life?' and he replied, 'I'm a representation of your anger and your insecurities, things you've never learned to deal with.'*
>
> *Since that dream, things have got much better. I still have some problems with Darren — by nature he's angry — but we're better at communicating these days and I realize now that, given the chance, I wouldn't get rid of him. He's an important part of me.*
>
> *This whole thing has been amazing — the potential of it all. One day I'd like to teach others how to lucid dream too.**

---

* Maxwell has since manifested that potential and you can hear him discuss his lucid dream experiences at his YouTube channel: TheRaRaRabbit.

Exercise: Hugging Your Demons

Inspired by Maxwell, which of your inner demons are you ready to hug, love and integrate into the wholeness of your being?

1. Decide upon which 'demon' (anything that obstructs your achievement of freedom) you want to invoke in your lucid dream and give it a name 'sexual shame' or 'fear of failure', for example.

2. Create a dream plan (*see page 231*) for meeting this particular demon.

3. Engage in your chosen lucid dreaming technique (*see page 221*).

4. In your next lucid dream, engage your dream plan by calling out, for example:

'Fear of failure, come to me!'

or

'Sexual shame, come to me!'

5. Be open to any new dream characters or changes in the dream that occur. Remember that sometimes your demon will manifest as a personification, but other times it may be more obscure.

6. Whatever manifests, actively embrace the manifestation with love, either through dialogue, affirmations of integration or, of course, a hug.

I've used this technique to meet 'rejected Charlie' (the demon of my fear of rejection) and those I've taught it to have used it to meet 'the source of my sadness' (the demon of their depression) and their 'sexual shame' (the demon of sexual trauma).

Whatever is preventing your experience of freedom, give it a name, call it into your dreams and embrace it. If you can do that, you have the potential to make revolutionary transformations to your mind.

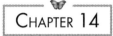

CHAPTER 14

DEATH: THE ULTIMATE SHADOW

*'Everybody should do two things in their lifetime: to observe
death and to consider what it will be like to die.'*

Alan Watts[1]

Each day 150,000 people do it and one day you will do it too,
but when was the last time you reflected on the fact that you
will die?

Death is the great equalizer, a shared commonality of human
experience. We will all die. Definitely and successfully. And yet
we never really prepare for it and we hardly ever talk about
it. Why is that? Fear mostly. But also denial, suppression and
shame. Death is, for many people, the greatest shadow and so
transmutation of our fear of it can reap the greatest benefits.

In the West, most of us live for about 1,000 months or so,
but of those 1,000 months how long do we spend preparing for
everything that those 1,000 months have been leading up to?
We need to begin redressing this imbalance and start waking
up to the reality of our own mortality. While we are alive, we
have a wonderful opportunity to prepare ourselves for death
and dying.

The reason death is scary is that we are not familiar with it
and we fear the unknown. With familiarity comes fearlessness.

Becoming familiar with death will not only take away our own fear, but also prevent us from projecting that fear onto the dying people we will inevitably come into contact with during our life. The best gift we can give someone who is dying is often not sympathy, it's familiarity.

Facing Death

We will all have to face death – we have no choice in that – but what we can choose is *how* to face it. Buddhist master Dzogchen Ponlop Rinpoche says, 'We have a choice: to prepare ourselves to face the most uncomfortable moment of our life or to meet that moment unprepared.'[2]

Thinking about death is not intended to make us feel sad, it's intended to help us overcome our sadness. The death of others is of course saddening and remembering those we loved who have passed away can be extremely painful, but I'm talking about contemplating your *own* death here, rather than other people's. If we are able to truly understand the mechanics and possibilities of death, our fear of it will start to dissipate and we can transform one of the densest shadows we hold.

Awareness of our own mortality also helps us to be more motivated and more compassionate human beings. With it, we bring the fear, shame, suppression and denial of death into conscious awareness and release the huge amounts of energy that we waste in trying to ignore it.

The Tibetan teachings tell us that we can transform our fear of death into a dynamic source of energy that can help us to wake up and live our life in a more beneficial and joyful way.

By waking up to death, we start to wake up to life. We become aware of the limitations of time. We realize that we don't have long to make our mark, to offer something of value to the human story. In the words of Dilgo Khyentse, 'On the day that you were born, you began to die. Do not waste a single moment more!'[3]

The Science of Mortality Awareness

Research published in the Journal of Applied Psychology and Social Science *in 2007 showed that 'death anxiety' led people to be 'more racist, nationalistic, homophobic and more likely to support violence against others'.[4] It explained: 'Self-esteem is the primary buffer which serves to protect humans from fear of their own mortality and when faced with fear of mortality, human beings will favour and draw closer to their own kind.'[5] This often results in increased levels of racism and tribalism.*

Luckily for us, though, becoming more conscious and aware of our own mortality integrates this 'death anxiety' and directly counteracts these harmful 'death-denying' symptoms.

A more recent study, conducted in 2016 by researchers at the University of Arizona in the United States, found that athletes who completed a questionnaire about death and their own mortality showed a '40 per cent improvement in their subsequent personal performance'.[6]

Another experiment in the same study asked basketball players to take part in a one-minute basket-shooting challenge. Half of the subjects received a subtle but conscious reminder of death: the researcher was wearing a T-shirt with a white skull on it along with other visual signifiers of mortality. Fascinatingly, 'those who'd seen the "death" T-shirt performed approximately 30 per cent better than those who hadn't'.[7]

Scientific proof that contemplating our own mortality makes us live more fully and effectively.

The Three Levels of a Good Death

From a Buddhist perspective, there are three levels that make a good death: dying with no regret, dying with no fear and dying with joy. Exploring these levels opens us up to the possibility that death is something that we can prepare for and so release the fearful shadow energy connected to it.

Dying without Regret

When I interviewed Lama Zangmo, the lama who runs the Buddhist centre where I live, about these levels of a good death, she began by telling me:

> The Buddhist teachings talk about three levels of practitioner: ordinary, medium and supreme. To die without regret is the first level of an ordinary practitioner. We want to die without feeling 'If only I had been kinder. If only I had made better choices. If only I had done more spiritual practice.'
>
> If we can die thinking, I have spent my life doing positive things. I have tried to extend myself and expand my mind, I have tried my best to help others, then that's great.
>
> Of course, we are going to make mistakes in our life – that's natural – but if we can look back on our life and say, 'Well, at least I don't have any really big regrets, I didn't spend my life doing very harmful things, I tried my best to be helpful, kind and compassionate,' then that's very precious. To die without regrets is a wonderful accomplishment.[8]

Dying without Fear

The next level up from this is when we are able to die not only without regret but also without fear. This is what is referred to in the teachings as a 'medium-level practitioner'.

Here you have trained your mind to the point where you have gained familiarity with death and impermanence to such a degree that your fear of it has dissolved. It takes a high level of awareness and stability to die without fear, but it is possible.

Lama Zangmo says that this comes not only from having familiarity with what happens when we die, but also having a level of mental stability developed through meditative practice that allows one to face death and impermanence fearlessly.

Dying with Joy

The final level is the level of 'the supreme practitioner', who dies without regret or fear and with joy. The Buddhist teachings tell us that we can die joyfully once we have recognized the nature of mind and have the awareness that there is no one there to die in the first place: the self is an illusion and the mind is beyond birth and death.

Of course, this reflects a high level of spiritual accomplishment and it is rare to die like this, but it is definitely seen among the meditation masters. These great practitioners are able to die not only with joy, but also while expressing genuine selfless compassion for those left behind.

Lama Zangmo says, 'They have achieved a level of realization where joy is constantly there, in every moment of life, and now in every moment of death. To die with this recognition of the illusoriness of all things is seen as the best kind of death. But if we are able to maintain any of these three levels at the time of death, that is a sign that we have applied the teachings very well.'[9]

Dying without fear and with joy can obviously take lifetimes to achieve, but dying without regret is something that we can all aspire to, so let's consider how we can do this.

Exercise: Things I Might Have Done Differently

In her book *The Top Five Regrets of the Dying*, Bronnie Ware, an Australian palliative care nurse, shares the most common regrets of her dying patients.[10] These can be summarized as:

- Not having the courage to be true to themselves

- Working too hard

- Not expressing their feelings

- Not staying in touch with their friends

- Not allowing themselves to be as happy as they could be

Inspired by these, we're going to explore what we would do differently in our own life if we knew that we were soon going to die.

Step 1
- Take a moment to come into an awareness of your breath. Just notice when you are breathing in and notice when you are breathing out.

- Notice three inhalations and exhalations before you begin.

Step 2
- Imagine that you are on your deathbed. Your mind is clear and you feel no fear.

  A nurse you particularly like and who is particularly kind is by your bedside and asks you, 'What things might you have done differently in your life?'

Step 3
- Take some time to consider the question. They don't have to be big things, just real things, personal to you.

- Try to think of at least three things that you might have done differently. For example, 'spent more time with my friends', 'said "I love you" more' and 'been more generous with money'.

Step 4

- Release the visualization and remind yourself that as you are not on your deathbed, you have the opportunity to actually *do things differently* from now on.

- Can you make a pledge to do those three things differently from now on so that you can die without regret whenever death comes?

- Take a moment to dedicate the beneficial energy of this exercise to all living beings.

My Journey into Death

When I was 17, I had what I later realized was a near-death experience caused by a drugs overdose.

I had the classic 'life flashing before my eyes' experience as I whizzed past what looked like photographs of my life in reverse chronological order. After passing childhood photos and then baby photos, my disembodied consciousness was sucked into a huge infinite black void. I would have been scared but there was no fear in this place. Fear and time were not present here.

Then a voice spoke to me. It was *my* voice, not the voice of God or the voice of judgement. It was me, and it said, in a totally neutral tone, 'Charlie, do you want to live or do you want to die?'

I yelled out, 'Live!' and proceeded to be sucked back through the tunnel while I heard a drum roll of increasing tempo, which I soon realized was the sound of my heartbeat as my cardiovascular system restarted.

That near-meeting with death left me with a fascination with death and dying, especially with helping those who are near to death themselves. Since 2008 I've been a member of the Bardo Group, which is the team of volunteers from the Buddhist centre where I live who offer practical assistance to those approaching the end of life. We help to organize the spiritual care, funerals and after-death prayers of people in and around London who have asked for our support.[11]

I've participated in quite a few of these funerals and am forever grateful for the opportunity to help others through what can be both their darkest and brightest times. One of the greatest privileges there is, and of one the best ways to integrate the shadowy fear of death, is to spend time with dying people.

We will all have to be around death at some point, so logically we should try to become as effective at dealing with it as possible. If our first experience of death is with someone to whom we are very close, do we really want that to be the time when we learn how to help a dying person? Surely it makes sense to learn about death beforehand and to take every opportunity to hone our skills at helping those who are dying.

If you are really serious about integrating your shadow, then death must be faced and embraced. So I urge you to consider doing all you can to beneficially habituate yourself to it, perhaps volunteering at a hospice or offering your time to a palliative care charity or checking out the brilliant Death Café movement, which invites you to talk about death over tea and cake.[12] Every year at the Kagyu Samye Dzong Buddhist Centre in London, we run the 'Embracing Death and Dying Day', a full day of talks, workshops and art exhibitions on the theme of death. Consider this your invitation to the next one.

If these suggestions are too much, then at least try to read about death, talk about death, celebrate death and definitely do the practical meditations around death that we will explore next.

Drowning Dogs

During the 1890s the Russian physiologist Ivan Pavlov was investigating salivation in dogs in response to being fed. In his famous study, whenever he gave food to his dogs, he also rang a bell so that the dogs came to associate the bell with food. After a while, he rang the bell on its own and, as you might expect, the dogs salivated, as they unconsciously associated the bell with food. Pavlov had programmed a new habitual pattern into their minds, sometimes called a 'conditioned reflex'. It's from this well-known experiment that we get the phrase 'Pavlovian response'.

What is less well known is that during the experiments Pavlov's laboratories in Leningrad were flooded by rising river levels. Pavlov's assistants came to the panicking dogs' rescue and although some dogs died, some of them were saved.

Their traumatic brush with death left the surviving dogs changed. Their conditioned reflexes had disappeared: they no longer salivated when the bell was rung. Their minds had been freed from their conditioning by the shock of facing their own mortality.

Hostage survivors, death-row inmates and those who have had near-death experiences often display a similar phenomenon. By facing our own death we can shift some of our own conditioning. We can get a taste of this deconditioning process too, simply by imagining that our death is coming soon.

Contemplating Our Death

> *'Of all the mindfulness meditations,*
> *that on death is supreme.'*
> **Buddha, in the Mahaparinirvana Sutra**

If you knew that you were going to die in one week from now, how would you spend your last seven days?

Considering this question, and crucially acting upon its response, is one of the most powerful shadow integration exercises there is. It draws into focus both the unfulfilled golden shadow potential that we neglect while also integrating the dark shadow fear of death.

Buddhist wisdom tells us that meditating on death and dying can help us to accept our own impermanence, stop wasting our time on meaningless activities and amplify our aspiration to wake up.

We have to plan for the future, of course, but if we can at least imagine that we have limited time then we might find that our life becomes much more alive.

We might start by saying what needs to be said too. Although we may have visions of loved ones gathered round our deathbed, listening intently as we say what needs to be said, palliative care expert Dr Angela Halley told me that:

> Most commonly there simply isn't time to reconcile what needs to be reconciled. In the last few hours many people can't even talk, let alone engage in the complex thought processes of reconciling relationships.
>
> Your body is diverting all of its resources to keep you alive. Dying is really not the time to say what needs to be said. That's why it's so important to do all the regrets and reconciliation stuff before we start dying. For most people, 'I forgive you', 'I'm sorry', 'Thank you' and 'I love you' are the four things that need to be said, so don't wait, say them now.[13]

Exercise: One Week Left to Live

This exercise can be found set to music and guided by my voice at www.charliemorley.com/shadowexercises under the title 'Seven Days Left to Live'.

Step 1

- Allow yourself to relax deeply.

- Focus on your breathing and count at least three deep but relaxed breaths.

Step 2

- If you knew that you were going to die in seven days from now, what would you do? Take some time to simply rest with the question in your mind.

  Who would you call? To whom would you apologize? Where would you go? What would you change in your life so that you could die at peace with the world? What niggly little conflict would you try to resolve? What wrong would you put right? What fear would you face? Be realistic, but be optimistic. If you knew that you were going to die in seven days, how would you spend your last week?

Step 3

- Now focus in on three or more specific things that you would do, say or make happen if you had one week left to live. They don't have to be big things, just personal to you. Decide on three or more things and take some time to note them down if you like.

Step 4

- If there is one thing on your list that you can realistically, safely and beneficially do within the next seven days of your life, will you do it? Why wait?

- If so, then I encourage you to do it. Don't wait until you are on your deathbed – make it happen now, within the next week of your life.

Step 5

- As always, dedicate your practice to the benefit of all beings.

Lucid Dreaming, Conscious Dying

*'Those who believe they have plenty of time get ready
only at the point of death. But isn't that far too late?'*
Padmasambhava, Tibetan Buddhist saint[14]

Tibetan Buddhism has a totally revolutionary view of death. It is not only something that is discussed openly, it is actually something that is trained for. It is believed that for a person who has prepared and practised, death can be the most important moment of their life, the moment of their full and complete enlightenment.

Lama Yeshe Rinpoche explained to me, 'Death is all part of the deal. It's not a disaster, it's an opportunity. Our physical form is just a vessel that we can change when we die. We get a new body – that's great! But there are other, more profound opportunities that come with death, such as the recognition of death, that can lead to spiritual awakening.'[15]

A full exploration of the after-death journey would fill an entire book – and, in fact, it has done in the form of the well-known *Tibetan Book of the Dead** and the dozens of commentaries that have been written on the text – but for now let's at least touch on the basics.

Buddhists believe, as Mingyur Rinpoche says, that the mind is an 'ever-changing stream of consciousness that never ceases, though it may inhabit many different physical bodies'[16] and that the mind does not die when the body dies. Instead, it is reborn.

As our body dissolves into death, with it dissolve the clouds of egocentric delusion that have stopped us recognizing our true Buddha nature. This dissolution of the body (and the ego that was so attached to it) reveals the mind in its inherently enlightened state.

---

* This text but it can be quite difficult to read, so if you are interested in exploring it further, I recommend Rob Nairn's *Living, Dreaming, Dying*, which is a Western psychological interpretation of the text, or Sogyal Rinpoche's classic, *The Tibetan Book of Living and Dying*.

Essentially, this means that death maximizes the opportunity for the mind to recognize its Buddha nature. This recognition can lead to full spiritual awakening. At death we don't need to go looking for enlightenment, we just need to have trained ourselves to recognize its display. How can we train for this? In large part through the conscious sleeping and lucid dreaming practices of dream yoga.

To Die, to Dream

Dreams and death are closely connected in Tibetan Buddhism and lucid dreaming is used by practitioners to prepare for their death and dying experience.

So what's the connection? The dying process is said to mirror that of falling asleep, so every night we're getting a trial run for death and dying. If we can master the art of falling asleep consciously (maintaining full awareness as we pass through the hypnagogic state into sleep), then we may be able to die consciously too, which is said to be one of the highest achievements of the spiritual path.

As mentioned before, Buddhists believe that once we die we are reborn, but that rebirth doesn't happen straight away. After death, we enter into something called the after-death *bardo** states, which are dreamlike intermediate states between death and rebirth, in which the mind displays itself in its fullest expression.

The dreamlike nature of the after-death *bardo* means that every time in our life that we recognize our dreams lucidly we are training for the conscious recognition of the dreamlike *bardo* too. According to *The Tibetan Book of the Dead*, if we can manage to recognize the dreamlike hallucinations of the after-death *bardo* state as manifestations of the mind, we have the possibility of experiencing full spiritual awakening.

---

* *Bardo* is a Tibetan word that means 'place in between' and is used to describe any transitional state of existence.

Basically, we practise lucid dreaming to prepare for lucid dying. And to die consciously or to become lucid in the after-death *bardo* is to open up to the potential of Buddhahood.

Lama Yeshe Rinpoche puts it best: 'If you can remember to recognize the dream consistently, then death means nothing to you, because you can recognize the death *bardo* as a dream, and then you can be with Buddha.'[17]

So for lucid dreamers, death is definitely not a disaster. For those who have mastered their dreams, death is the final opportunity to wake up.

In Your Dreams...

The training for a conscious death includes many deep and profound practices, but here is a brief summary of four trainings recommended within Tibetan Buddhism to prepare for a more conscious death.*

Four Trainings for Conscious Dying

1. *Learn to meditate:* At certain points during the death and dying process the true nature of mind is displayed, but it is said that only those who have familiarized themselves with the mind's true nature and stabilized their minds through meditation practice while alive will have any chance of recognizing this display at death.

2. *Learn lucid dreaming:* Part of the after-death *bardo* experience is said to be dreamlike and so those who have mastered the art of lucid dreaming may be able to recognize these *bardo* visions as displays of their own mind and with that recognition gain enlightenment in the *bardo*.

---

* If you are interested in exploring the spiritual and practical preparations for death in more depth, check out the 'Lucid Living, Conscious Dying' workshop that I run with my friend Sergio Magaña.

3. *Embrace angels and demons in your dreams:* At one stage of the after-death journey, the mind displays itself in huge magnificence through the form of what are called the 'peaceful and wrathful deities'. These will appear as awesome archetypal energies of both seemingly angelic and demonic appearance. Those who have trained themselves to habitually embrace both their inner angels and demons in their lucid dreams (and lucid nightmares) may habitually do the same here, which in this stage of the *bardo* would mean embracing their fully enlightened state.

4. *Try to fall asleep consciously:* When we die, we experience what is called 'the dissolution of the elements', which is a progressive process of elemental energies dissolving into each other. This has certain mental and physical correlates that can be recognized as they occur, allowing the dying person to know exactly what stage of death they are at.

    When we fall asleep at night, the same process occurs, so by being more conscious of our descent into sleep and the changes that occur within our body and mind during this process, we are training our capacity to do the same at death.

These four practices can take a lifetime to truly master, but one practice that we can all do to prepare for our death in the meantime is to review our life.

The Life Review

> 'Let us not wait to review our lives on our deathbed.
> Let us finish our business before our lease is up.'
> **Stephen Levine**[18]

Looking back over the past and taking stock of it all is a brilliant way to integrate past shadows, become aware of the story of our life and make friends with the past. It's also a brilliant way to prepare for death and to release the shadow of fear that we hold around it.

With so much shadow material stored in forgotten memory and unconscious habits, the life review allows us to spot shadow traits and emotional patterns that have recurred unconsciously throughout our life. This is a powerful way to use past shadows to integrate our present ones.

The life review process asks us to document every significant memory from every five-year chapter of our life. We bear witness to what changed us, what broke us, what helped us, who loved us and what we made of it all. We write down not just what happened, but also how we felt about what happened.

It's far better to witness, 'download' and digest these memories now, in a structured, compassionate way, than let them fester in our shadow, blocking our psychological growth and causing unseen anxiety in our psyche. As the memories arise, we need do nothing more than bear witness with love and acceptance for their energy to be integrated.

Consciously bearing witness to our past helps liberate regret and shame from the dark shadow while highlighting potential in the golden one. We remember our forgotten mistakes with forgiveness and our forgotten light with joy.

The First 32 Years

I first did the life review when I was 32 years old, during a three-month meditation retreat. Each day for a week I would spend an hour or so documenting one five-year chapter, listing every major life event, significant memory, noteworthy moment, emotional trauma and forgotten joy. I would then spend another hour reading it through and allowing myself to really enter into each memory and feel the feelings completely, knowing that, as you too know now, 'feeling the feeling leads to healing'.

As I reviewed my life, I was amazed to see how much I'd done, how lucky I'd been and what an abundance of joy had been offered to me. I remembered lost loves, forgotten friends and seemingly insignificant events that had created huge opportunities in my life. I sent love to those who had helped me and felt gratitude for the gifts I'd been given. I was amazed at how much joy I'd simply forgotten.

But I was also shocked and ashamed by some of the stuff I'd done – the horrible things I'd said to people, the harsh way I'd treated others, the soft hearts I'd trampled on, and the kindness that I'd never appreciated. It was painful at times and I cried a lot.

As I did this, I trusted in what Stephen Levine says in his brilliant book *One Year to Live* – that if we allow ourselves to really feel into the pain of those we hurt, while sending them our love and compassion, both parties receive healing. And so I prayed and cried and laughed and sent healing energy to dozens of people who may not even have remembered me, but whom I wanted either to apologize to or to thank.

As I went on reviewing each five-year chapter, I made friends with my blame and my shame, and I gave thanks to those who had helped me. When I'd finished and I looked back over my first 32 years, I saw beyond doubt two truths: i) meeting life with love makes life easier; and ii) everyone is always just trying their best.

Avoid the Rush

As well as offering you the chance to bear witness to your life and to integrate the shadows of your past, the life review has some slightly more esoteric benefits too. One of these is regaining the psychic energy that is often tied up in the storage or suppression of past memory.

Every interaction we have ever had has left an imprint on our energetic system. This imprint is stored as a memory. Each memory of each one of these encounters requires energy to keep it alive and so over the course of a lifetime we lose huge amounts of energy doing this. If we can liberate the energy it takes to store these memories by remembering and downloading them onto paper, we regain this energy.

Doing the life review may also offer the possibility of having more profound dreams. Dreams are the most common way that past memories are revealed, and so practices similar to the life review are used in shamanic lineages as a way to free up space in the dreaming mind, which helps foster more profound dreams and to facilitate lucid dreaming.

The library of our unconscious mind is constantly being inventoried and so anything stored in our memory will be revealed as part of this inventory at one point or another: in our dreams, in our unseen shadow projections and finally, if not witnessed before, in our dying process.

Reviewing our life may also review our experience of death. The well-documented life flashing before our eyes phenomenon found in many near-death experiences is caused in part by the fact that the dying process forces us to witness all the events in our life as our mind downloads its content. It seems that the unconscious mind is recording everything we have ever done and at death that recording is played back to us in time-lapse fashion.

Those who witness that display but survive are often deeply moved by the experience and start living very differently, based on taking stock of what they saw. By doing a life review, we can start watching that recording now and begin taking stock while we are still living and thus avoid the last-minute rush of death.

When Rob Nairn was diagnosed with PTSD from his time in the Rhodesian Bush War 40 years ago, not even his decades of meditation practice could stop the tsunami of repressed trauma from flooding his psyche. And yet even in the depths of his suffering he told me, 'At least I'm releasing this stuff now. Far better now than waiting until death. Now I can witness it consciously at least.'

And with that I realized that while his meditation practice didn't make him immune to PTSD, it had given him a truly profound understanding of death, suffering and the nature of the mind which helped to lead him into a full recovery.

Exercise: The Life Review

This exercise is a great way to prepare for death, let go of your past and gain the freedom to live your life with more awareness and joy.

It can either be done in one day or spread over several, but before you begin here are my top tips on the process:

1. *Feel into the memory.* Don't just explore what happened but also how you felt about what happened.

2. *Use photos.* Photo albums can be used to help spark your memory, but use them only after you have exhausted your mental recollection of a certain chapter.

3. *Be a loving witness.* Try to look back over your life without judgement or blame.

4. *Don't grasp too hard.* What you can't remember is often as telling as what you can. There's no need to strive to find memories – just allow as many as want to reveal themselves to do so. This is a gentle practice – powerful but gentle.

5. *Mine for gold.* To integrate your golden shadow, be sure to recall the successes, achievements, loves and inspirations of each chapter. But also be aware of your unlived life: in what areas of life have you limited the full expression of your gold?

6. *Look to your dreams.* A practice that recapitulates so many forgotten and unconscious memories is bound to have an effect on your dreams, so be sure to stay open and attentive to them on the nights that follow this exercise.

7. *Allow it all.* Aspire to house all your memories under a roof of love held up by the three pillars of acceptance, friendliness and kindness, but when anger or regret arise, as they naturally will, give them equal space to display themselves too.

8. *There's no need to lift the lid.* If you know that there is trauma or abuse in your past, feel free to simply acknowledge these memories if and when you encounter them without feeling any pressure to intentionally lift the lid on them.

And I want to leave you with one last idea: *kintsukuroi.* This is a Japanese term meaning 'golden repair' and refers to the art of repairing broken pottery with a kind of resin made with powdered gold. When a pot cracks, rather than being seen as a fault, it is embraced as an opportunity to make it more beautiful and, with the addition of gold, literally more precious than before.

As you look back over your life story and see the cracks of regret or fractures of remembered heartache, take the opportunity to fill those cracks with the gold of love and compassion. This will make your story even more precious than before.

Step 1

• You might like to set a strong intention for this practice as a way to illuminate your life story with compassion.

Step 2

• Spend time documenting every memorable event from your birth to the present day, in five-year chapters – every significant moment, noteworthy memory, joy, challenge, friendship, upset and achievement.

You can do this as a long list or as a spider diagram or mind map. Use words or pictures and work on paper or digitally, either is fine.

You don't have to work chronologically. Memories from one chapter may arise while you are working on another, so feel free to skip between chapters.

Accept all memories, great or small. The fact that you remembered a particular event during this exercise is testament to its significance.

Take it slowly and playfully. I advise exploring the happier memories of each chapter first as a way of building a solid foundation of gratitude.

Spend anything from 20 minutes to several hours documenting each five-year chapter, but be sure to give yourself enough time to sit in forgetfulness too. Long-lost memories may take time to surface.

Step 3

- At the end of each chapter, read through what you've written and simply bear witness to it.

- Whenever you come across a happy memory, take time to imagine the person or situation that was central to it and send them your love and gratitude. Bring them into your awareness and say, either mentally or out loud:

    Thank you. May you be happy and well. I send you my love.

- Similarly, when you come across a painful memory, you may like to imagine the person or being that was central to it and if you can, bring them into your awareness and say, either mentally or out loud:

    I see you and I let you go. May you be happy and well. I send you my love.

- For a deeper practice, try sending *tonglen* healing (*see page 172*) to the person or situation from your past. For a situation, use exactly the same method as the standard *tonglen*, but imagine the situation that you want to heal rather than a specific person.

Step 4

- Once every few five-year chapters, take time to reflect on what occurred over those years. The energy of the past is integrated through the act of friendly observation, so simply witness the memories without judgement.

- You might like to reflect on the themes of each chapter by asking yourself:

    - *'What are the dominant emotional themes of this period?'*

    - *'How much of this chapter was I aware of before?'*

    - *'Are there any dark shadow traits being created or played out in this chapter?'*

    - *'Are there any golden shadow traits being created or played out in this chapter?'*

Step 5

- Once you have completed the life review, you might like to explore the following questions:

    - *'When were the times that I felt most alive? And what has that taught me about myself?'* (Robert Holden once told me: *'Aliveness is an intelligence. It's life telling us, "This is the feeling of you living me fully."')*

    - *'When in my life have I been following my joy and living a life I've loved? And when in my life have I been living a life I didn't love?'*

    - *'What lessons have I learned from my life?'* Pick five top lessons if you can.

    - *'Where have I felt most in my element and most authentic? And when have I felt most lost, most inauthentic?'*

Step 6

- Take a moment to dedicate all the goodness in your life to the benefit of all beings.

Step 7

- You may like to share some or all of your life review with a friend or therapist. This can be a very beneficial way to complete the process.

    Simply by engaging in this process, you will find an energetic integration of your shadow automatically beginning to take place. In fact, by this point in the process it may already have done so.

You have done what most people only get to do on their deathbed. You have reviewed your life story and in doing so you not only get to integrate what would have to be presented for integration at death, you also get to co-author the rest of it.

One of the people I consulted while writing this book is a brilliant psychotherapist called Jacqueline Harper. When we were discussing how shadows are created by the stories we tell ourselves about who we are, she said something that struck me as quite profound: 'We say that it's the events of our lives that form the story of ourselves, but in adulthood it's actually the story about ourselves that invites the events of our lives. If we change our story, we change our life.'[19]

Confession and Self-forgiveness

As we remember the ups and downs of life, we are given a second chance – not to put a situation right perhaps, but at least to put our conscience right.

Your life review may have reminded you of times when you did things that you would rather forget, but in the Buddhist tradition some of the most essential things to do before we die are to confess, to release anything that we are still holding onto and to forgive ourselves. Why wait till death? Let's do so now.

This is not about trying to get rid of our guilt, rather releasing the stranglehold that it so often has on us. We can decide that we have been holding on to the guilt and shame for long enough and that we now release it and offer its energy to the universe, while accepting the forgiveness that has always been available to us.

In Buddhism we confess and accept forgiveness not out of fear of damnation, but simply because if we remain constricted by guilt and shame, we are less able to address our behaviour and move on. If we can openly confess what has happened and accept forgiveness from ourselves, without searching for it from others, we can be more helpful human beings.

To forgive ourselves is to choose to identify with self-love rather than with self-shame. It allows us to stop identifying with our biography and helps us see that we are more than what we have done, however seemingly unforgivable our actions may have been.

Confession and the forgiveness it can lead to are two of the most powerful ways to release shadow content. To confess to our mistakes is to acknowledge the shadow and to forgive ourselves is to release the shadow of the blame and shame that lie within it.

Dr Alex Lickerman from the University of Chicago says, 'Though confessing by no means guarantees a release from guilt, it's likely the only way to make such a release possible. Certainly, confessing may not move the person you've hurt to forgive you, but it will open up an even more important possibility: that you will be able to forgive yourself.'[20]

So often we either hide from the shame of past wounds or we cannot stop picking at the scab of guilt that lies over them. Forgiveness, however, for ourselves and others clots the blood of guilt and turns open wounds into healing scars.

Sometimes we feel that forgiving ourselves is somehow undeserved and that we are helping the person whom we wronged by maintaining our guilt and shame. The opposite is true, for it is our guilt that energetically connects us to the wronged person, and so when we release our guilt with forgiveness, we also release that person too.

Exercise: Self-forgiveness

Why wait till our deathbed to release our guilt and accept the forgiveness that has been available to us all along? Let's do it now – we have dragged this bag around for long enough.

Step 1

- Sit in front of an image of an embodiment of compassion and wisdom, or imagine one. It could be Jesus, Buddha, Mother Mary, a source of white light or whatever you feel represents wisdom and compassion.

- Take a moment to come into an awareness of your breath. Just notice when you are breathing in and notice when you are breathing out.

- Notice three inhalations and exhalations before you begin.

- Really try to feel the presence of the embodiment of compassion.

Step 2

- Speaking directly to the image, take the time to confess fully to your role in the situation about which you still hold self-resentment or shame. Speak out loud if you can.

  Use this opportunity to confess fully and completely to what occurred. Allow yourself to feel your feelings fully.

  This is not a trial and you are not being judged. There is no need to defend or justify yourself.

  Allow yourself to confess fully to your role in the situation without the addition of either blame or defence.

Step 3

- Once you have said all that you need to, remind yourself that your true nature is divine and that the essence of who you are is untainted by whatever you have done.

- Now imagine that the enlightened being to whom you have confessed smiles lovingly at you and perhaps even says, 'You are forgiven. You are loved.'

- As they smile at you, healing light shines out from them and dissolves into you. As it does, it purifies you of any shame and lack of forgiveness. (It doesn't matter if you can't visualize this clearly – just imagine and trust.)

Step 4

- Now say out loud if you can:

    I release my shame. I forgive myself. May I be happy. May I be well.

- Repeat this three times.

Step 5

- Dedicate the beneficial energy of the meditation to all sentient beings.

Gratitude

The Life Review allows us to let go of the pain of our past, and to also become aware of those who helped us in our past. These people are not only vital guides and catalysts of our potential, but they are also often golden shadow reflections of ourselves.

These people often see a reflection of their own inner light in ours and so they know what we are truly capable of before we do. And yet how many of these people have we taken the time to thank, truly and fully, for what they have done for us? How many of these catalysts of our true potential have we acknowledged as such?

To take time to do so is to pay homage to the golden shadow and to liberate even more of its untapped energy into our psyche.

Exercise: The Gratitude Letter and Visit

In this exercise you will acknowledge and pay homage to the people who have helped you by writing them a gratitude letter and then, if possible, thanking them face to face. Through this you not only offer thanks to those who have helped you, but also integrate your golden shadow and ask it to offer you its energy even more fully than before.

Step 1

- Take a moment to come into an awareness of your breath. Just notice when you are breathing in and notice when you are breathing out.

- Notice three inhalations and exhalations before you begin.

Step 2

- Select one important person from your past who saw your golden potential before you did and who may have helped you to manifest that potential too.

- Take some time to relive the memory of exactly what this person did for you and how it helped to manifest your particular golden shadow potential.

Step 3

- Write a short letter to that person, which you are willing to share with them, describing how they helped you and thanking them for their support.

  You don't have to mention shadow work if you feel it may complicate things. The power of this exercise comes from paying homage to the beneficial potential that they helped you to unlock and then by showing gratitude to *their* inner light for doing so.

Step 4

- As soon as possible, find a way to communicate the contents of your letter to that person. If you can, go and visit them and share it face to face. That would be best. If that's not possible, then you can do it over the phone or send them the letter or email it. If they are no longer alive, read the letter out loud while directing the words to their memory.

- Allow the other person to respond unhurriedly and give yourselves time to reminisce about the events in question and how they impacted upon both of your lives.

  If they feel too shy to respond or if they block the process, that's fine. The process doesn't require reciprocation to work.

The first time I did this practice was with Rob Nairn. After reviewing my life, it became clear to me that my entire career could be traced back to the opportunity he had given me nine years before.

After he read the gratitude letter (he was teaching at the time, so I couldn't share it face to face), he came over to me with watery eyes and said, 'That was the kindest thing anybody has ever written me.'

We then sat and reminisced about what I had written in the letter.

Since then I've written gratitude letters and made gratitude visits to estranged friends, teachers, guides, family members and those who helped me in ways I had yet to fully thank them for. None of those relationships have ever been the same again. Once you open up and truly show people your gratitude, your hearts are entwined forever.

CONCLUSION

*'And where we had thought to find an
abomination we shall find a god.'*

Joseph Campbell[1]

I was going to start this conclusion by saying something like
'Even by the end of this book we have barely scratched the
surface of the shadow...' but when I thought about it, I realized
this wasn't actually true. If you have really engaged with all the
practices in this book, explored what's in your bag, dropped
your masks, found the lotuses in your mud, learned to lucid
dream (be kind with yourself on this one, as it can take a
while), looked into your ancestral past, healed your parental
shadow, integrated your sexual story and done the rest of the
practices, then you have definitely more than scratched the
surface of the shadow. And yet, as I'm sure you can feel, the
shadow is so deep and so dark and so rich that integrating it
fully is a lifetime's work.

So, apart from being sure to actually *do* the practices in
this book (rather than just read through them), how can you
keep on with this work? At the back of the book I've added a
Resources section (*see pages 251–253*) where you'll find details
of online courses and workshops. This is a good place to start.

Moving Forwards into Darkness

There's a well-known quote from Carl Jung that says: 'One does not become enlightened by imagining figures of light, but by making the darkness conscious.'[2] This quote actually has a second part to it that is rarely included. He says that doing so is disagreeable to many people and thus not popular. The often sanitized dilution of modern-day spirituality proves him right: so many of us would rather drown in denial than to truly see ourselves. But just as we can only see the stars at night, so we must go into the darkness if we want to see our light.

In the Gospel of Thomas, Jesus said, 'What you do not bring forth will destroy you,' which is an invitation to bring our shadows into the light. Buddha, Mohammed, Moses and Jesus all had to face their inner demons, darkness and devils before they could know the glory of godliness. What makes us think that we can avoid what they could not?

The shadow contains aspects that can be potentially harmful to ourselves and others, but 'the destructiveness of the shadow is largely a function of the degree to which we refuse to take responsibility for it'.[3] When we refuse to illuminate our dark side, we are living on dangerous ground, because if we allow it to fester, it will grow more powerful, whereas if we bear loving witness to it, we befriend it and transmute its energy.

The safest and greatest gift we can give the world is an integrated shadow. Over the two years of writing this book, the world has changed in many huge and sometimes terrifying ways, and never has the time for shadow integration been riper than now. Never has there been a better moment to integrate our own darkness and own our golden light. The world needs shadow workers now more than ever.

It's been said that the aim of shadow work is not changed behaviour, but changed understanding, out of which a change in behaviour arises.[4] Whether through changed understanding or behaviour, writing this book has definitely changed me for the better and I hope that reading it has in some way done the same for you.

Five Tips for Illuminating the Darkness

To help continue your beneficial change, here are five tips for moving forwards on the path of shadow integration in everyday life:

1. Move Towards the Places That Scare You

One of my mentors, the shamanic practitioner Ya'Acov Darling Khan, once asked his Peruvian Achua shaman how to work with his shadow, to which he replied, 'Whatever frightens you, move towards it. Get to know what makes you afraid.'

Within every fear lies a shadow, and within every shadow lies the gold of our innate vitality. Fear is often the sound of the ego resisting the integration of the shadow. We make a comrade out of our shadow every time we go through an initiation of fear. So I ask you, 'What are you scared of in everyday life and how can you explore that fear safely?' Whether it's singing in public or picking up a house spider, working at integrating our fears in everyday life not only integrates the shadow, but also moves us towards fearlessness: not the absence of fear, but the courageous befriending of it.

2. Every Day, in Every Way, Embrace Your Magnificent Messiness, with Love

Shadow work is not about fixing ourselves (we were never broken in the first place); it is about showing up authentically, and unconditionally loving ourselves and others in all our magnificent and very human messiness.

3. Be Fascinated by Projection

Most of us are constantly projecting and most of the time we are totally unaware of this. So much of the harm that we do to ourselves and others is based on mistaking our projections for the truth. If we could learn to recognize our projections, we would become kinder to ourselves and others. This realization can save our relationships.

Every day, every time you are triggered, try to pause and ask yourself, 'Am I projecting?' and 'What aspect of my shadow is this person or situation showing me?' Allow these questions to create a buffer zone between the trigger and your response.

4. Don't Forget to Plant Lotus Seeds

Lotus flowers cannot grow from polished crystal, they grow from the sometimes foul-smelling soil of the human condition. Shadow work will not protect us from the inevitability of old age, sickness and death, nor will it armour-plate our heart so that it never breaks. But it will allow us to enter these places with more love and more awareness and perhaps even allow us to plant lotus seeds there instead of just drowning in the mud.

5. Look to Your Dreams

By opening up to our dreams, we are opening up to the shadow. When we dream, we are a captive audience for the displays of the shadow, so try not to sleep unconsciously through the show. Being lucid is the greatest sign of respect for the shadow, for it says, 'I want to know you. I am ready to embrace you.' But just remembering, documenting and becoming more conscious of your dreams is also a great step forwards.

Owning Our Gold

The mythologist Joseph Campbell famously told his students to *follow their bliss*. Later in life, frustrated by the misinterpretation of his words, he said that he should have told them to follow their *blisters*.

The journey to the mountaintop is an adventure. It is a hero's journey into the golden shadow and we must be prepared for challenges.

Integrating our golden shadow is perhaps the hardest part of all shadow work. It is far easier to label our blinding inner light as separate from ourselves and project it outside. And with this comes the creation of gods and gurus.

But however powerful, infinite and astonishing the content of our golden shadow, we must try to accept that it is not the power of another person working through us, but our own divine nature calling out to be seen.

The egocentric mind's dominance relies on a constant maintenance of the status quo. It will strive just as hard to keep us away from our golden shadow as it does to deny our dark one. Owning our gold is a direct challenge to its dominance.

Owning our gold will change everything. If we truly accept that the seed of full spiritual awakening is already germinating within us, then how can we possibly go on living the way we have been? Perhaps that's why it's such a threat to our egocentricity?

Suppressing or refusing to befriend the dark shadow may lead to outbursts of anger, jealousy or self-sabotage, but what happens if we refuse to face our golden shadow? Psychologist Abraham Maslow is clear about this. He says, 'If you deliberately plan to be less than you are capable of being, then I warn you that you will be unhappy for the rest of your life.'[5]

So, when it's your time to shine, as it always is, shine fiercely and unapologetically. We are happiest when we are expressing our golden potential. For what is happiness but freely expressing our inner light while rejoicing in the light of others?

Five Tips for Owning Your Gold

Here are five tips for continuing to integrate your golden shadow into everyday life:

1. Keep It Playful

Some people lose faith in their ability to own their gold by taking the whole thing too seriously and then giving up when they don't step into its full manifestation overnight. For example, if part of your unmanifested potential is a love of dance, don't sign up for advanced ballet straight away. Instead, perhaps go to an 'ecstatic dance' class where you can release your gold in a playful and safe way. If it's your spiritual gold that you want to integrate, then don't go straight into a 10-day silent Vipassana retreat, but perhaps start with a drop-in meditation class. Keep it playful and take your time.

2. Make Friends with Your Past

The heavy clouds of who we used to be often prevent us from seeing the bright sunlight of our golden potential. When I first started teaching, it was fear that someone with a past like mine (sex, drugs and hip hop) shouldn't be teaching that was the greatest hindrance to me stepping into my gold. If you can befriend your past and start to direct your light forwards, your golden potential will manifest with far greater ease.

3. Step into Your Light

I know it's terrifying, but just experiment with it. Bit by bit, start choosing to do things differently. Just small things: start going to those dance classes you've always dreamed of, start wearing the clothes you like, start applying for that job that you've always wanted and little by little you'll find that you're moving into your light already.

Whenever you are challenged to step into your light or take an opportunity that challenges you to shine, maybe you can think: *How would I respond to this situation if I were free of my shadow of fear?* and perhaps even, *If this were a lucid dream, would I still say no?*

4. Be Kind

It's been said that our compassion arises from our very fallibility and that 'love takes root in the soils of human error',[6] so be kind to yourself as you progress on the path and know that everyone else is probably working with similar shadow stuff too.

Every time we are unkind or believe that we are more important than everyone else, we further our separation from love and solidify our shadow content. But the moment that we see others as equally important or even more important than ourselves we seem to short-circuit the operating system of both the egocentric mind and the shadow that it has created.

5. Share Your Gold

There is a Buddhist saying: 'When we share our light with others, we do not diminish our own light. Rather, we increase the amount of light available to all.'[7] So, share your golden shadow potential with others, inspire them to do the same and help to nurture and encourage those who are yet to see their gold within themselves.

The essence of all these tips is summed up by this quote from my golden shadow archetype, Hafiz:

One regret, dear world,
That I am determined not to have
When I am lying on my deathbed
Is that
I did not kiss you enough.[8]

Last Words

It's been said that 'the essence of bravery is being without self-deception'.[9] Shadow work asks us to wake up and to enter into that bravery, to see ourselves clearly and to accept the shadows of who we are while being open to the true magnificence of who we will become.

Your work with the shadow doesn't stop here and you shouldn't want it to stop here either, because our goal is not to get rid of the shadow, but to lovingly befriend it and to recognize it as a benevolent force that points us towards our own greatness. By doing so, we not only open up to the possibility of showing love to all aspects of ourselves, but also to becoming a more authentic version of ourselves, a version which is and always was a fully awakened Buddha.

Shadow work asks us to 'love the strength and the weaknesses, to love the being lost and the being found, to love the sleep and the awakening'.[10] And it is awakening that this work can lead to. I'm definitely not there yet, and I often find myself still stuck in the mud, desperately clutching at lotuses, but I'm closer than before, as you are too, dreaming through darkness together.

So let us wake up and start dreaming our reality into existence, moving into the freedom of shamelessness found in Rumi's field, beyond all notions of dark and light or wrong and right.

From that place we can love it all, both the brilliance of our Buddha nature and the Magnificent Messiness of the human condition. For shadow work, as you now know, is all about love.

LUCID DREAM INDUCTION TECHNIQUES

The following techniques have been abridged from my book *Lucid Dreaming: A Beginner's Guide.*

If you are interested in exploring lucid dreaming and Mindfulness of Dream and Sleep* in depth, then I recommend my first book, *Dreams of Awakening*, but for a quick-start guide to getting lucid, the techniques in this appendix are all you need.

Lucid dreaming can take months to stabilize and even then you may only be having a few fully lucid dreams a month, so take it slowly and relax into the process. Lucid dreaming is just one of the many ways you can integrate your shadow, and apart from the practices in chapters 9, 10, 11 and 13, it is *not a prerequisite* for the techniques in this book.

Once you have started keeping a dream diary you can move on to spotting dream signs, the first of our lucid dream techniques.

Exercise: Dream Signs

If I blindfolded you and took you into a bakery, I reckon you'd still be able to tell me where you were, right? Although you couldn't see the bakery, its smells,

---

* Mindfulness of Dream and Sleep is a holistic approach to lucid dreaming and conscious sleeping that is not just about learning how to lucid dream, but rather how to use all areas of falling asleep, dreaming and waking up for spiritual and psychological growth.

sounds and atmosphere would be enough to indicate your whereabouts. You've smelled the aromas of a bakery and experienced its atmosphere so many times that you're able to recognize one even through a blindfold.

In the same way, we can come to recognize the dream state, even when blindfolded by non-lucidity. How? By getting to know its unique sights, sounds and atmosphere. This forms the basis of spotting dream signs.

A dream sign is any improbable, impossible or bizarre aspect of dream experience that can indicate we're dreaming. Most people's dreams are full of dream signs – things as far out as talking dogs and dead relatives or as subtle as dreaming of being back at school. Basically, if it's something that doesn't usually occur in waking life, it may well be a dream sign.

There are many different categories of dream sign, but I classify them into three main groups:

- *Anomalous:* random, one-off anomalies such as talking fish or ninja babies.

- *Thematic:* dreamlike themes or scenarios such as being back at school or being naked in public.

- *Recurring:* dream signs that have appeared multiple times. These are a real boon for lucid dreamers.

One of the most important reasons for keeping a dream diary is to record and chart our personal dream signs. But how does all this lead to lucid dreams? By acknowledging our particular dream signs in the waking state we create a lucidity trigger that'll be activated the next time we see that dream sign, thus triggering lucidity.

Five Steps to Spotting Dream Signs
1. Once you've recalled and written down your dreams, read back through them, on the lookout for dream signs.

2. If you dreamed that you were walking down a street and saw Barack Obama standing next to a blue dragon, then your dream signs would be 'Barack Obama' and 'blue dragon'. Unless you're Michelle Obama, of course, in which case seeing Barack Obama wouldn't be a dream sign because he's a feature of your everyday life. The blue dragon, however, would still be a dream sign.

3. If you've dreamed of a blue dragon several times, this would be a recurring dream sign. Recurring dream signs mean recurring opportunities to become lucid!

4. Once you've pinpointed your dream signs, make a determined effort to be on the lookout for them in future. This effort will permeate your dreams, and eventually you'll start recognizing dream signs while you're dreaming and become lucid. Set a strong intention to recognize them the next time they show up in your dreams!

5. Before bed, remind yourself again and again: 'The next time I see Barack Obama [or whatever your particular dream signs are], I'll know that I'm dreaming!' Then, when you next dream about your dream sign, the lucidity trigger will be activated, making you spontaneously think, *Barack Obama? Aha! This is a dream sign, I must be dreaming!*

Exercise: Reality Checks

One of the most common entries into a lucid dream is simply spotting a dream sign and becoming lucid. But sometimes, even though you've spotted a dream sign and are sure that you must be dreaming, the rest of the dream looks so realistic that you simply can't accept that you're in a dream. This is when you need something called reality checks.

Dr Stephen LaBerge and the researchers at the Lucidity Institute in California have scientifically verified that there are certain things that are virtually impossible for the human mind to replicate consistently within the pre-lucid dream state (the state just before you're lucid), and so these can be used to confirm reliably whether or not you're dreaming. Reality checks will almost always be performed in the pre-lucid dream state, because if you're conscious enough to think, *I should do a reality check*, then you're often almost lucid already.

There are lots of different reality checks, but I'll take you through some of my favourites:

- Looking at your outstretched hand twice in quick succession without it changing in some way.

- Reading text coherently twice without it changing in some way.
- Using digital or electrical devices without them changing or malfunctioning in some way.

During a dream, the brain is working flat out to maintain the projection of our elaborately detailed dreamscape in real time, and although it's amazingly good at this, once pre-lucid (just before becoming fully lucid) it often struggles to replicate the detail of an intricate image (such as a piece of text or an outstretched hand) twice in quick succession. So, if we try to make it engage in such a replication, it will provide a close but imperfect rendering, and it's the acknowledgement of this imperfect rendering that makes us lucidly aware.

Let's explore those three reality checks in more depth:

Looking at Your Hands

If you think you might be dreaming, but you're not 100 per cent sure, look at your outstretched hand within the dream, then quickly look away and look back at it again. Alternatively, watch your hand as you flip it over and back again. Either way, your brain will usually struggle to reproduce an identical projection of your hand, so on second glance it may be a strange shape, perhaps missing a finger or two, or look dappled or transformed.

When you look at your hand twice in a row, the dreaming brain tries its best to reproduce exactly the same image, but it doesn't quite have the processing speed to do so perfectly. The variations are multiple, but the result is singular: if you really expect your hand to change, it will change.

I know the hand-checking thing can sometimes be a bit hard to imagine, so let me break it down for you:

- You're in a dream, something weird happens and you think you might be dreaming. You look at your dream hand, flip it over (with the expectation that it'll change if you're dreaming) and when you flip it back, it probably will have changed in some way.

- The dreaming mind is very creative (I've seen my hand turn into a baby elephant and grow three new fingers!), but it's not very good at replicating precise detail. Hands are pretty detailed, so it really struggles to replicate them to order.

Reading Text

Within a pre-lucid dream it's virtually impossible to read any text coherently twice in succession. LaBerge's research laboratory found that in lucid dreams text changed 75 per cent of the time as the dreamer was reading it and 95 per cent of the time on second reading.

So, when you're in a dream and you think you might be dreaming, try to read something. The text will often be unintelligible, move around as you're reading it, or in some cases just fade away altogether. All these are signs that you're dreaming.

Using Digital or Electrical Appliances

Just as the dreaming mind struggles to reproduce text, it also struggles with the highly detailed screen of a smartphone or a computer, which will often seem blurred and transformed in a pre-lucid dream as the dreaming mind struggles to project it accurately.

I know it sounds crazy, but in a dream it's often impossible to read a digital watch, successfully operate any form of digital or electrical appliance or switch a light on and off. This works on the principle that if you flick a light switch within a dream, you're asking the dreaming mind to project an exact replication of the dreamscape but in a totally different light and shadow setting, literally at the flick of a switch. This is something that it finds almost impossible to do.

Remember: If you think you might be dreaming but want to be 100 per cent sure (before you try to fly through the sky), look at anything with a detailed pattern – such as your hand – twice in a row and if it changes you'll know for sure that you're definitely dreaming.

Exercise: The Weird Technique

Although opportunities for reality checks will often crop up in your dreams naturally, they're usually only engaged once you spot a dream sign and need confirmation of your present reality. You can, however, actively hasten the process by getting into the habit of conducting reality checks while you're awake. This is the basis of the Weird Technique – a deceptively simple method through which I have the majority of my lucid dreams. Here's how to do it:

- As you go about your daily life, whenever something weird happens, or whenever you experience synchronicity, *déjà vu*, a strange coincidence or any other type of dreamlike anomaly, ask yourself, 'Am I dreaming?' and then answer this question by doing a reality check.

- By doing reality checks during the daytime (whenever something weird happens), you will soon see this new habit reappearing in your dreams. But when you check your hand in your dream, it will change and you'll become lucid!

- If you spend your day packing boxes, what might you dream about that night? Packing boxes, right? And so by spending your day asking yourself, 'Am I dreaming?' and then doing a reality check, that night you may well dream about doing that too. But when you dream about doing it, the reality check will indicate that you're dreaming and lead to lucidity.

Okay, wait, what do I do again? Whenever you see something weird or unexpected in your daily life, take a moment to think, *That's weird. Could I be dreaming right now?* Then perform a reality check and, as long as your hand doesn't grow an extra finger or morph into a baby elephant, you can be sure that you're definitely not dreaming. This sets up a habit that'll crop up in your dreams too, but in your dreams the hand *will* change and you will become lucid.

Exercise: Hypnagogic Affirmation

The hypnagogic state is the transitional state between waking and sleeping, so I'm pretty sure you can imagine how this technique works. As you fall asleep through the hypnagogic state, mentally recite a positive affirmation of your intent to gain lucidity. As we've learned, the hypnagogic state is very similar to the hypnotic state, so if we apply a suggestion or affirmation within it, we may find that it has the potential to work with hypnotic effect.

Five Steps to Hypnagogic Affirmation

You can do this technique as you first fall asleep at night, but for best results practise it after an early-hours wake-up about five or six hours after you went to bed. At this time the hypnagogic will lead directly into the dream state. Whenever you practise it, though, the important thing is to saturate your sleepy consciousness with the strong aspiration to have a lucid dream. Here's how:

1. Take some time to create an affirmation of your intent to have a lucid dream such as, 'I recognize my dreams with full lucidity' or 'Next time I dream, I'll know that I'm dreaming', or whatever phrase you feel best encapsulates your intention to get lucid.

2. As you enter the hypnagogic state, continuously recite this affirmation in your mind.

3. Try to recite your affirmation with real feeling and gusto – this is vital, because without determination, this technique simply won't work.

4. The important thing is not so much that you're repeating the affirmation right up to the point at which you enter the dream (although that would be great), but more that you saturate your last few minutes of conscious awareness with the strong intention to gain lucidity.

5. Aim for your affirmation to be the last thing to pass through your mind before you black out.

The last few hours of our sleep cycle are also when we enter dreams most easily from the waking state. This makes it prime time for lucid dreaming. While you can have lucid dreams in the first few hours of your sleep cycle, the dream periods will be short and your mind may be quite groggy. However, in the last few hours you'll not only have longer dream periods but also a fair few hours of sleep under your belt, so your mind will feel fresh and ready to engage in lucidity.

Basically, the first half of the night is mainly deep sleep with short dream periods and the second half is mainly dreaming with not much entry into deep sleep.

Exercise: Falling Asleep Consciously

For many people, falling asleep consciously, or FAC, is the Holy Grail of lucid dreaming practice, but it's really not such a big deal. Although it can take a long time to master it, I've taught hundreds of people this technique and seen them apply it successfully within a few weeks – or even on the first night of practice.

FAC combines elements of a well-known lucid dreaming technique called WILD (wake-initiated lucid dream) with a few of my own methods and a twist of meditative awareness. The aim is to pass through the hypnagogic state and enter REM dreaming sleep without blacking out or losing consciousness. FAC is both incredibly simple and often incredibly elusive, and involves letting your body and brain fall asleep while part of your mind stays aware.

I advise that you practise this technique after briefly waking in the last few hours of your sleep cycle, when you will enter REM dreaming straight from the hypnagogic state. When you first fall asleep, it may be 80 minutes before you enter your first dream period, but if you wake yourself in the early hours (either naturally or with an alarm) and then fall back asleep, you'll enter dreaming within about 15 minutes. For this technique it's a case of the more direct the entry into the dream state, the better.

I have three favourite versions of the FAC technique that I teach. Let's look at each one individually.

Five Steps to Hypnagogic Drop-in

To enter the dream state lucidly, be like a surfer: paddle through the hypnagogic imagery* and 'drop in' to the wave of the dream lucidly. If you have a good sense of mental balance and awareness, then this is the technique for you!

1. After at least four and a half hours of sleep, wake yourself up and write down your dreams. Then set your intent to gain lucidity, close your eyes and allow yourself to drift back into sleep.

2. As you enter the hypnagogic state, gently focus your mental awareness on the hypnagogic imagery and simply float through it, allowing it to build,

---

*   These are the dreamy hallucinations and mini-dreams that often accompany the hypnagogic state.

layer upon layer. The key here is to maintain a delicate vigilance without blacking out and being sucked into the dream state unconsciously.

3. Don't engage the hypnagogic imagery that'll arise, but don't reject it either. Just lie there watching it until the dreamscape has been formed sufficiently for you to drop into it consciously. If you feel yourself blacking out, just keep bringing your focus back to the hypnagogic imagery. It'll continue to build, layer upon layer, until it starts to coalesce into an actual dreamscape. This is a wonderful thing to witness.

4. As the dreamscape solidifies, you might feel a slight pull or a sensation of being sucked forwards. This is an indication that the wave of the dream is now fully formed. In surfing terms, you're on point break.

5. If you can just stay conscious for a few more moments and are ready to take the plunge, you'll find yourself dropping into the wave of the dream with full lucidity.

Five Steps to Body and Breath

If you have good body awareness (perhaps you like to dance, or do body work or yoga), you may find that this version of the FAC technique is the one for you. It involves scanning your awareness through your body as you drift into sleep and enter the dream lucidly.

1. Some time after at least four and a half hours of sleep, wake yourself up and write down your dreams. Set your intent to gain lucidity, close your eyes and allow yourself to drift back into sleep.

2. As you enter the hypnagogic state, gently focus your mental awareness on the sensations in your body and the breath flowing through it. The hypnagogic imagery will still arise, but rather than focusing on it, as in the hypnagogic drop-in technique, this time focus on the sensations in your body. If you feel yourself blacking out, just keep bringing your focus back to the sensations of the body and breath.

3. You might find that systematically scanning your awareness through the body works well for this. Alternatively, you might choose simply to allow bodily sensations to attract your attention as they arise. Becoming aware of the contact points of your body on the bed works well too.

4. At some point you may actually feel the body paralysis that accompanies REM sleep. There's no need to freak out if this happens – it simply means that you're on the doorway of the dream.

5. Once you've scanned your body, or allowed your attention to be aware of particular sensations, become aware of your whole body as it lies in space. Hold your entire body within your awareness and allow your mind to remain lucid as the dream forms out of the hypnagogic and you enter it lucidly.

Five Steps to Counting Sleep

This version of the technique isn't particularly meditative, and it doesn't call for much body awareness either, but it does require the ability to maintain a sense of reflective awareness as you abseil down into the dream. By combining counting with a repeated question (or reflection) as you go through the transition from wakefulness into dream, you can maintain your awareness fluidly.

1. Some time after at least four and a half hours of sleep, wake up fully and write down your dreams. Set your intent to gain lucidity, close your eyes and allow yourself to drift back into sleep.

2. As you enter the hypnagogic state, continuously question your level of consciousness as you count yourself into dreaming. For example: *One: Am I dreaming? Two: Am I dreaming?* and so on. I prefer to use: *One: I'm lucid? Two: I'm lucid?* for this technique, but use whatever feels right for you.

3. For the first few minutes the answer to the question will probably be *No, I'm still awake!* but once you've counted into the twenties, it'll probably be, *I'm now in the hypnagogic state.*

4. If you can make it into the thirties or forties, or even fifties, without blacking out, the answer may become, *Almost! The hypnagogic state is starting to solidify!* Limit your count to double figures, though – once you start getting above 100, you may have overshot your mark and be too awake by then.

5. The eventual aim is to answer the question 'Am I dreaming?' with something like, *Sixty-one: Am I dreaming? Hang on…yes, I'm dreaming! I'm lucid!* as you find yourself fully conscious within the dream.

Exercise: Lucid Dream Planning

Planning a lucid dream is a lucidity technique in itself, because when we set a strong intention to do something in our next lucid dream, we not only start to attract the causes and conditions needed to make that dream manifest, but we also create an expectation of becoming lucid.

On my workshops I teach three main stages to lucid dream planning: i) writing a dream plan; ii) drawing a dream plan (the dreaming mind works in images, so this helps) and iii) creating a *sankalpa* (a Sanskrit term which means 'will or purpose'), or statement of intent. The steps below include them all.

Five Steps to Lucid Dream Planning

1. Draft some ideas of what you'd like to do in your next lucid dream. What question would you like to ask? What activity would you like to engage in? What part of your shadow would you like to interact with?

2. Once you've decided what you want to do, begin to formulate your dream plan. Start with 'In my next lucid dream I…' and then write a description of what you want to do once lucid.

3. Next, draw a little picture of your dream plan in action. I just use stick men and speech bubbles when I draw my dream plans, but if you're artistic then of course feel free to do more.

4. Now write your *sankalpa*, or statement of intent. This should be a pithy statement that sums up the essence of your dream plan. For example, if your dream plan is a complex description of how you want to meet your inner child and embrace it with loving kindness, your *sankalpa* might be the much more concise 'Inner child, come to me!' Your dream plan can be as long and detailed as you like, but I recommend that you keep your *sankalpa* short and sharp.

5. The final step occurs when you next find yourself in a lucid dream. Once you get lucid, recall your dream plan, say your *sankalpa* out loud and then carry out your chosen dream plan.

There are dozens more lucid dreaming techniques that we could explore, but these will get you started and are definitely sufficient to begin inducing lucid dreams if practised diligently.

Exercise: Settling, Grounding, Resting with Support

This mindfulness exercise is based on the Mindfulness Association UK's 'Settling, Grounding, Resting with Support' technique.

Step 1

- Sit on a hard-backed chair or on a cushion cross-legged on the floor. Make sure that you're comfortable and have your back straight. Buddha said, 'When the cup is still, the water is still,' so try to stay quite still if you can, and if you need to itch or stretch, do so mindfully.

- Keep your eyes open or closed – either is fine. Breathe through the nose or mouth – either is fine.

- Settle the mind by focusing in a very relaxed way on your breath. Breathe in a little more deeply than normal and then gently release the breath.

- You might like to keep in- and out-breaths equal in length, breathing in to a count of three or four and breathing out to a count of three or four.

- When you have thoughts, just let them go freely, without attempting to reject or engage them. Simply leave them alone and guide your focus back to the breathing and counting.

- After a few minutes, begin to focus a little more on the out-breath and drop the counting. Notice that as you release the out-breath, the body relaxes a little. This is how you settle the mind.

Step 2

- Now you ground the mind in the body by dropping any regulation of the breath and bringing your focus onto your body. Simply become aware of all the bodily sensations being experienced. That's all.

- You might find that a systematic scanning of the body works well for this. To do this, scan your awareness throughout your body quite slowly, starting from your feet and ending at your head, then return to the feet and do it again.

- Alternatively, you might choose simply to sit and allow bodily sensations to command your attention as they arise. Becoming aware of the contact points of your body on the floor or seat and noticing any points of bodily tension or relaxation works well.

- Become aware of how your body is supported by the ground beneath you. Feel the weight of your body creating pressure where you're sitting. Let go into the unconditional support of the ground. Be aware of how gravity roots you.

- Once you've scanned your body or allowed your attention to be aware of particular sensations, then become aware of your whole body as it sits in space. Hold your entire body within your awareness.

- Allow yourself to experience how your body exists in space and is surrounded by space. This is how you ground the mind in the body.

Step 3

- Once you have grounded the mind in the body for about five to 10 minutes, move on to resting. You rest the mind by letting go of any sense of focus on the body or the breath.

- Simply rest. Don't try to meditate, just sit there. Give up any idea of trying to do anything. Simply be aware and in touch with whatever comes to you, with a panoramic awareness.

- The point of resting is to allow the mind to relax deeply and to let go of any sense of striving, struggling or trying to achieve. It is not directed in any way, but involves simply being in the moment.

- See if you can rest in this way for one or two minutes at first. This is the highest form of meditation – a flash of the mind's natural unlimited openness. Because our mind is very unsettled, this state is usually very elusive to us. However, here we momentarily taste this freedom, so we sense its possibility.

Step 4

- When you notice that your mind is becoming involved with thoughts (which might happen after just a few seconds), you can move on to resting with sound as the support.

- There are many mindfulness supports you could use, such as the breath or bodily sensations, but I've found that sound is a particularly accessible support for most people.

- For sound to become the support for your mindfulness, simply focus your attention on any and all the sounds that you can hear. Allow sound to anchor your awareness in the present moment.

- Don't reject or engage any of the sounds you can hear, just open up to whatever sounds are naturally present around you: cars outside, footsteps in the next room, the rustling of your clothes, even your own heartbeat.

- Try to hear rather than listen. Listening is often goal-driven and preferential, whereas hearing is more relaxed and open. Just hear and be aware of sound.

- Whenever you drift away into thought and realize, *Oh no, I'm thinking!* just very gently, with kind patience and without irritation, return your attention to sound. Remind yourself that there is nothing wrong, that your distracted mind is giving you an opportunity to exercise your muscle of mindfulness, that's all.

Step 5

- Just sit there, knowing (and hearing) what is happening while it is happening, and each time you drift off, gently bring your mind back to the awareness of sound.

- Spend about 10 to 15 minutes on resting the mind like this with sound as the support.

- At the end of your session, be sure to dedicate the beneficial energy that you will naturally have generated for the benefit of all beings.

The above practice might take between 20 to 30 minutes, but if you want to, you can extend it for as long as you like, spending the greater portion of it in the 'resting' and 'resting with support' stages.

A SELECTION OF LUCID DREAMS

The following lucid dreams are taken directly from my own dream diaries. They have been transcribed exactly as written, but I have taken the liberty of editing out any insignificant or boring bits. The 'prep. before bed' parts are lists of the techniques, causes and conditions that may have led to that particular lucid dream.

Ancestor Lucid Dream

6 August 2016

I dropped into the dream consciously from the hypnagogic. Once lucid, I started calling out to the dreamscape, 'I love you! I love you all! You are all loved!' as an offering of love to the dream.

Then I remembered my dream plan to do lucid dream ancestor work, so I started calling out, 'Ancestors, I love you! I send love to my ancestors!' which felt really strong and quite emotionally moving.

As I walked through the dream calling this out, I passed a mirror and went to see what I looked like in it. I didn't really expect it to have anything to do with the ancestor affirmation I'd called out, but when I looked in it I saw something so weird: my reflection was wearing women's clothes. It was me but in women's clothes and I actually looked quite pretty. It should have been funny, but it felt so natural. I couldn't work out what it meant and, in fact, I felt so comfortable looking like that and so beautiful that I thought for a moment that the dream might be telling me that I was actually transsexual! Then I looked more closely at the reflection and realized that I was dressed like Jay (my dead grandma). In fact, I was Jay – that's why it felt so natural.

Once I realized that, the transformation became more complete and I saw that I had her black shoulder-length hair and was wearing one of her fifties-style dresses. As I looked at my reflection, I appreciated her beauty and then, still lucid in the dream, I realized what this meant: I had called out for my ancestors and the dream had replied by showing me that they existed within me. They existed in my own reflection. Every time I looked in the mirror they were there with me – my lineage, my blood.

I then left the mirror and carried on walking through the dream, calling out, 'I love you, my ancestors! I send love to my ancestors!'

Then I woke up into a false awakening (a dream within a dream) and then woke up for real.

Prep. before Bed

Fell asleep reciting lucid dream affirmations ('Next time I'm dreaming, I'll know that I'm dreaming') and visualizing Lama Yeshe Rinpoche in my throat chakra. Plus, had been recently exploring my ancestry.

Meeting the Essence of My Shadow

30 May 2016

Amazing lucid dream! I got lucid from a false awakening and once lucid, I called out, 'I want to meet the essence of my shadow!'

Then a young woman who seemed to be a kind of helpful dream guide appeared and said that she would take me to him. I was told he was the most powerful shadow aspect there was and the sum total of the shadow.

As she took me down some corridors I began to feel a bit scared in light of what she'd told me and I asked her, 'Is he scary?'

She said, 'No, he's not scary. You'll be fine.'

She guided me to a room and inside there was the biggest snake I had ever seen! Its head was over three feet wide and its coiled body filled the room. I had a moment of fear and the snake felt my shock and instantly transformed into human form, so that I could talk to him more easily.

I bowed before him and sat at his feet in reverence. There was no way I was going to hug him – he wasn't a regular shadow aspect, he was the very essence of shadow, and not just mine, but perhaps everyone's, so I wanted to bow to him, not hug him.

I asked him, in the light of how powerful he seemed, 'Am I ready for this level of shadow work?'

He replied, 'Why take on more when you have so much you're currently working on? But you are working well, so there is a possibility that you are ready for this level.'

The lucidity began to slip and I woke up.

Prep. before Bed

First session of sleepover retreat in Ashland, Oregon, USA. High confidence and lots of conscious sleeping due to snorers!

Jesus Lucid Dream

23 November 2014

In the last session on the retreat I got lucid from falling asleep consciously. I appeared in a dream version of my old house at Grove Crescent (in Kingston upon Thames, southwest London). I remembered my dream plan and then walked out of the front door and called out, 'Jesus Christ! I want to meet Jesus Christ! Jesus, come to me! I love you!'

I then floated up into the night sky and I thought I saw his face appear in the sky, but suddenly my eyes closed, and instead of going dark, everything was brilliantly bright and everything became white light.

I was hanging suspended in space surrounded and encompassed by bright white light, wondering what all this had to do with Jesus. Then it hit me: this is what Jesus Christ is — infinite bright white light. Jesus is pure light!

Prep. before Bed

Running sleepover retreat at a Catholic nunnery, which is full of images of Jesus, hence the dream plan.

Very Realistic Lucid Dream with Golden Shadow Affirmations

2 June 2016

In the dream I was in my bedroom, and I saw that it looked really different so I thought, That's weird, why does my bedroom look so strange? Then I looked out of the window and the view was totally different, so realized I must be dreaming.

Once I knew I was dreaming I flew out of the window to explore outside. I started picking things up and marvelling at how amazingly realistic everything looked and felt. I picked up a crystal that I found, and the texture was perfect and just like in waking life. I could reach for the leaves on a tree, and even feel the breeze of the wind blowing against my bare arms. I took a moment to appreciate how crazy it was that the dreaming mind could even create a cool breeze like that.

Then I remembered my dream plan to connect with Lama Yeshe and so I flew into the sky and started chanting, 'Om Mani Peme Hung, Lama Yeshe Rinpoche! Om Mani Peme Hung, Lama Yeshe Rinpoche!' As I chanted a new scene appeared ahead of me: a young monk who I sensed was ill and needed healing. I touched his head and did hands-on healing while I chanted, and this seemed to make him transform in some way. I realized that maybe my inner young monk (whatever that represents) needed healing.

I then felt the lucidity start to slip so I started calling out (almost like a song) a golden shadow affirmation: 'I am love, I am joy, I am beautiful,' over and over.

Then I saw two other dream characters and started singing, 'You are love, you are joy, you are beautiful!' to them.

Prep. before Bed

I read The Tibetan Book of the Dead and also took high-strength B vitamins and magnesium before bed. I also had jetlag from a USA return flight.

Shadow hugging and spiritual practice lucidity

4th March 2015

I became lucid after seeing that the room I was in looked really weird, and then doing a reality check.

Once I knew I was dreaming, I saw that there was some sort of scary, dark, formless shadow aspect in the room, and initially I just yelled at it to leave. I didn't have time for shadow work when I had an important dream plan – saying prayers for my friend Tamas, who had just died. The shadow aspect disappeared straight away, but then I felt a bit bad to have dismissed it so I went out of the room and found it in the corridor. It had transformed into a scary, but also scared-looking, woman so I said mantras for her and hugged her.

Then I flew out of the window and started reciting Amitābha mantras and prayers, while I visualized Amitābha Buddha in the sky before me and also tried to send the energy of the mantras to Tamas in the after death bardo. It was so stable and clear, and the mantras started to gain power very quickly. As the dream approached a crescendo I felt a bliss almost like a sexual orgasm, and then woke up from the intensity of it.

Prep. before Bed

I slept at Samye Ling Monastery after having taken Tamas's body into the shrine. Very high energy. I'd had several lucid dreams before this so felt on a roll. Felt a bit of pressure to get lucid so that I could try to help Tamas.

REFERENCES

Introduction

1. Rumi, 'The Great Wagon', trans. Coleman Banks, *The Essential Rumi*, Quality Paperback Book Club, 1995, p.36

Part I: Meeting the Shadow

1. James Hillman, 'The Cure of the Shadow' in *Meeting the Shadow: Hidden Power of the Dark Side of Human Nature*, eds Connie Zweig and Jeremiah Abrams, Jeremy P. Tarcher, 1990, p.242

Chapter 1: Our Dark and Golden Shadows

1. Robert A. Johnson, *Owning Your Own Shadow*, HarperSanFrancisco, 1991, p.17

2. Stephen A. Diamond, PhD, www.psychologytoday.com/blog/evil-deeds/201204/essential-secrets-psychotherapy-what-is-the-shadow

3. Ya'Acov Darling Khan, in conversation with the author, October 2016

4. Rob Nairn, in conversation with the author, December 2015

5. Rainer Maria Rilke, *Letters to a Young Poet*, trans. Stephen Mitchell, Burning Man Books, 2001

6. www.goodreads.com/author/quotes/17297.Marianne_Williamson

7. David Richo, *Shadow Dance*, Shambhala Publications, 1999, p.3

8. Michael Fordham, *Jungian Psychotherapy*, John Wiley & Sons Ltd, 1978, p.5

9. Marie-Louise von Franz, www.youtube.com/
    watch?v=OvL00iQ0ao4

10. www.samyeling.org/quotes/

11. Stephen Batchelor, foreword, Rob Preece, *The Psychology of
    Buddhist Tantra*, Snow Lion Publications, 2006

12. The ancient Greek aphorism 'Know thyself' was inscribed
    outside the Temple of Apollo at Delphi and was seen as the
    essential aim of all philosophies.

Chapter 2: The Benefits of Shadow Integration

1. C.G. Jung, quoted in D. Patrick Miller, 'What the Shadow
    Knows: An Interview with John A. Sanford' in *Meeting the
    Shadow: Hidden Power of the Dark Side of Human Nature*, eds
    Connie Zweig and Jeremiah Abrams, Jeremy P. Tarcher, 1990,
    p.21

2. www.thesap.org.uk/resources/articles-on-jungian-psychology-2/
    about-analysis-and-therapy/individuation/

3. Clive Holmes, in conversation with the author, 2016

4. Professor Paul Gilbert, Mindfulness Association Annual
    Conference, Samye Ling Monastery, Eskdalemuir, UK, 2015

5. Sogyal Rinpoche, *The Tibetan Book of Living and Dying*, Rider,
    1993, p.245

6. www.greatergood.berkeley.edu/article/item/why_racism_is_
    bad_for_your_health/

7. www.huffingtonpost.com/ed-and-deb-shapiro/how-your-mind-
    affects-you_b_7204636.html

8. Thich Nhat Hanh, www.goodreads.com/quotes/548044-
    awareness-is-like-the-sun-when-it-shines-on-things

Chapter 3: Constructing the Shadow

1. Brené Brown, PhD, *Daring Greatly*, Gotham Books, 2012, p.60

2. Rob Nairn, in conversation with the author.

3. www.ns.umich.edu/new/releases/8332-study-illuminates-the-
    pain-of-social-rejection

4. Brown, op. cit., p.68

5. Cited in the introduction to Part 10, 'Owning Your Dark Side through Insight, Art and Ritual', in *Meeting the Shadow: The Hidden Power of the Dark Side of Human Nature*, eds Connie Zweig and Jeremiah Abrams, Jeremy P. Tarcher, 1990, p.272

6. Quoted in the Talmudic tractate *Berakhot* (55b)

7. David Richo, *Shadow Dance*, Shambhala Publications, 1999, p.14

8. Ken Wilbur, 'Taking Responsibility for Your Shadow' in Zweig and Abrams, op. cit., p.274

9. Professor Geoffrey Lantz, Skype conversation with the author, December 2016

10. Wake Forest University, www.sciencedaily.com/ releases/2010/08/100802165441.htm

11. Lama Surya Das, *Tibetan Dream Yoga*, audio CD, Sounds True, 2001

Chapter 4: Childhood Shadow

1. Quoted in *Peter's Quotations: Ideas for Our Time*, ed. Laurence J. Peter, Bantam Books, New York, NY, 1977; 1979 edition, p.25

2. Robert Holden, in conversation with the author, autumn 2016

3. Mingyur Rinpoche, *The Joy of Living*, public talk DVD, recorded in Hartford, USA, 9 August 2007

4. www.webmd.com/balance/features/science-good-deeds?page=2

5. Ibid.

6. Quoted in the *Big Issue*, 15 October 2015, p.25

7. www.psychologytoday.com/blog/compassion-matters/201305/4-ways-overcome-your-inner-critic

8. Ibid.

9. Robert Firestone, quoted in John Bradshaw, 'Taming the Shameful Inner Voice' in *Meeting the Shadow: Hidden Power of the Dark Side of Human Nature*, eds Connie Zweig and Jeremiah Abrams, Jeremy P. Tarcher, 1990, p.274

10. Robert Holden, in conversation with the author, October 2016

11. Ibid.

12. Ibid.

13. www.ncbi.nlm.nih.gov/pubmed/17466400

14. http://learningtoforgive.com/research/stanford-northern-ireland-hope-1-project

15. http://sm.stanford.edu/archive/stanmed/1999summer/forgiveness.html

16. Tim O'Brien, *The Things They Carried*, Mariner Books, 2009, p.13

17. Pema Chödrön, *The Places That Scare You*, Shambhala Publications, 2001; HarperElement edition, 2003, p.113

Part II: Befriending the Shadow

1. http://our-ireland.com/william-butler-yeats-quotes/

Chapter 5: Mindfulness Meditation

1. www.insightmeditation.org/the-buddha-s-words-on-mindfulness-3

2. Yongey Mingyur Rinpoche, *Turning Confusion into Clarity: A Guide to the Foundation Practices of Tibetan Buddhism*, Snow Lion Publications, 2014, p.32

3. Lama Yeshe Rinpoche, in conversation with the author.

4. www.scientificamerican.com/podcast/episode.cfm?id=mediation-correlated-with-structura-11-01-22

5. www.sciencemag.org/news/2014/07/people-would-rather-be-electrically-shocked-left-alone-their-thoughts

Chapter 6: The Masks That We Wear

1. www.goodreads.com/quotes/6849187-tear-off-the-mask-your-face-is-glorious

2. www.ted.com/talks/johann_hari_everything_you_think_you_know_about_addiction_is_wrong

3. www.forbes.com/sites/erikkain/2011/07/05/ten-years-after-decriminalization-drug-abuse-down-by-half-in-portugal/#26811fa63001

4. James Hillman, 'The Cure of the Shadow' in *Meeting the Shadow: Hidden Power of the Dark Side of Human Nature*, eds Connie Zweig and Jeremiah Abrams, Jeremy P. Tarcher, 1990, p.242

5. Yongey Mingyur, *Turning Confusion into Clarity: A Guide to the Foundation Practices of Tibetan Buddhism*, Snow Lion Publications, 2014, p.179

6. Tai Situpa Rinpoche, www.youtube.com/watch?v=oyCUsK0VQM8

7. Dzogchen Ponlop, *Mind Beyond Death*, Snow Lion Publications, 2006, p.165

8. Sogyal Rinpoche, *The Tibetan Book of Living and Dying*, Rider, 1993, p.53

9. James Low, *Being Guru Rinpoche: A Commentary on Nuden Dorje's Terma Vidyadhara Guru Sadhana*, Trafford Publishing, 2006, p.250

10. Dzogchen Ponlop, op. cit., p.165

11. William A. Miller, 'Finding the Shadow in Daily Life' in Zweig and Abrams, op. cit., p.39

12. Rob Preece, *The Psychology of Buddhist Tantra*, Snow Lion Publications, 2006; 2012 edition, p.14

13. Robert Bly, *A Little Book on the Human Shadow*, HarperCollins, 1988, p.49

Chapter 7: 'No Mud, No Lotus'

1. www.goodreads.com/work/quotes/26376035-nonviolence-the-transforming-power

2. http://tricycle.org/magazine/beautiful-storm/

3. http://time.com/3967885/how-trauma-can-change-you-for-the-better/

4. www.researchgate.net/profile/Kate_Hefferon/publication/23185195_Post-traumatic_growth_and_life_threatening_physical_illness_A_systematic_review_of_the_qualitative_literature/links/543ebd8e0cf21c84f23cb038.pdf

5. www.psychologytoday.com/blog/stronger-the-broken-places/201610/post-traumatic-growth

6. http://time.com/3967885/how-trauma-can-change-you-for-the-better/

Chapter 8: Revolutionizing Nightmares

1. Rob Preece, *The Psychology of Buddhist Tantra*, Snow Lion Publications, 2006; 2012 edition, p.14

2. Justin Havens, in conversation with the author, August 2016

3. A.L. Zadra and R.O. Pihl, 'Lucid dreaming as a treatment for recurrent nightmares', www.ncbi.nlm.nih.gov/pubmed/8996716

4. Ibid.

5. J. van den Bout, 'Lucid dreaming treatment for nightmares: a pilot study', *Spoormaker* Vol. VI(1), 2006; www.ncbi.nlm.nih. gov/pubmed/1705334112

6. European Science Foundation, 'New Links between Lucid Dreaming and Psychosis Could Revive Dream Therapy in Psychiatry', *Science Daily*, 29 July 2009; www.sciencedaily.com/releases/2009/07/090728184831.htm

7. www.ncbi.nlm.nih.gov/pubmed/23838126

8. www.drweil.com/drw/u/ART00521/three-breathingexercises.html

9. Tenzin Wangyal Rinpoche, *The Tibetan Yogas of Dream and Sleep*, Snow Lion Publications, 1998, p.103

Chapter 9: Lucidly Embracing the Shadow

1. Lama Yeshe Rinpoche, in conversation with the author, summer 2016

2. 'Lucid dreaming: a state of consciousness with features of both waking and non-lucid dreaming', http://sciconrev.org/2009/10/lucid-dreaming-a-state-of-consciousness-with-features-of-both-waking-and-non-lucid-dreaming/

3. Max-Planck-Gesellschaft, 'Lucid dreamers help scientists locate the seat of meta-consciousness in the brain', *Science Daily*, 27 July 2012. Retrieved 10 August 2012 from www.sciencedaily.com/releases/2012/07/120727095555.htm.

4. D. Erlacher and T. Stumbrys. Heidelberg University, Germany, and University of Bern, Switzerland, and M. Schredl, Central Institute of Mental Health, Mannheim, Germany, 'Frequency of lucid dreams and lucid dream practice in German athletes, imagination, cognitions and personality', *Imagination, Cognition and Personality*, Vol. 31(3) 2011–12, pp.237–46

5. Robert Waggoner, *Lucid Dreaming: Gateway to the Inner Self*, Moment Point Press, 2009, p.17

6. Saljay Rinpoche, quoted in Yongey Mingyur, *Turning Confusion into Clarity: A Guide to the Foundation Practices of Tibetan Buddhism*, Snow Lion Publications, 2014, p.152

7. Lama Yeshe Rinpoche, in conversation with the author, July 2016

8. Glenn H. Mullin, *Six Yogas of Naropa: Tsongkhapa's Commentary Entitled: A Book of Three Inspirations*, Snow Lion Publications, 2005

9. Traleg Kyabgon Rinpoche, *Dream Yoga*, five-disc DVD set, E-Vam Buddhist Institute, 2008

Chapter 10: Golden Shadow Lucidity

1. www.telegraph.co.uk/pets/news-features/the-legend-of-arthur---the-dog-that-followed-me-100-miles/

2. Quoted in Daniel Ladinsky and Shirazi Hafiz, *I Heard God Laughing: Poems of Hope and Joy*, Penguin Books, reprint edition, 2006, p.1

3. Ibid., p.73

Part III: Transmuting the Shadow

1. Joseph Campbell, *The Power of Myth*, Bantam Doubleday Dell, 1989, p.120

Chapter 11: The Ancestral Shadow

1. www.goodreads.com/quotes/15579-what-lies-behind-us-and-what-lies-before-us-are

2. Stephen Victor, in conversation with the author, October 2016

3. Steve Biddulph, *Manhood*, Finch Publishing, 1995, p.43

4. Lama Choyin Rangdrol, in conversation with the author, summer 2015

Chapter 12: Exploring the Sexual Shadow

1. Keith Witt, *Shadow Light*, Integral Publishers, 2016, p.162
2. Sergio Magaña, *The Toltec Secret*, Hay House, 2014, p.85

Chapter 13: The Peacock and the Poison

1. Quoted by Ian Baker, in conversation with the author, February 2016
2. Geshe Lhundrup Sopa, *Peacocks in the Poison Grove*, Wisdom Publications, 1996
3. Rob Preece, in conversation with the author, October 2016
4. Ian Baker, op. cit.
5. www.taramandala.org/about-kapala-training/the-process/
6. www.rigpawiki.org/index.php?title=Tonglen
7. www.taramandala.org/about-kapala-training/the-process/
8. Quoted in Patrul Rinpoche, *The Words of My Perfect Teacher: A Complete Translation of a Classic Introduction to Tibetan Buddhism*, Yale University Press, 2010, p.305
9. www.taramandala.org/about-kapala-training/the-process/
10. Lama Tsultrim Allione, in conversation with the author

Chapter 14: Death: The Ultimate Shadow

1. www.azquotes.com/quote/1078453
2. Dzogchen Ponlop Rinpoche, *Mind Beyond Death*, Snow Lion Publications, 2008, p.1
3. www.tricycle.com/insights/city-dreams
4. Cited by John Underwood, Embracing Death and Dying Day speech, Samye Dzong, London, November 2016
5. Schimel, Hayes, Williams and Jahrig, http://insight.cumbria. ac.uk/2208/1/Hoelterhoff_ATheoreticalExploration.pdf
6. www.medicalnewstoday.com/articles/313836.php
7. Ibid.
8. Lama Zangmo, in conversation with the author, June 2016
9. Ibid.
10. www.inspirationandchai.com/Regrets-of-the-Dying.html

11. www.london.samye.org/services/bardo-group

12. Visit www.deathcafe.com for more info.

13. Dr Angela Halley, Embracing Death and Dying Day, Samye Dzong, London, November 2016

14. Quoted in Sogyal Rinpoche, *The Tibetan Book of Living and Dying*, Rider, 1993, p.14. HH the Dalai Lama says, 'It is the actual point of death that some of the most profound and beneficial inner experiences come about,' and even in the case of a person with the highest spiritual awakening, full and complete enlightenment (called *parinirvana* in Sanskrit) only comes at the actual point of death.

15. Lama Yeshe Rinpoche, in conversation with the author

16. Yongey Mingyur Rinpoche, *Turning Confusion into Clarity: A Guide to the Foundation Practices of Tibetan Buddhism*, Snow Lion Publications, 2014, p.117

17. Lama Yeshe Rinpoche, in conversation with the author

18. Stephen Levine, *A Year to Live*, Bell Tower, 1997, p.69

19. Jacqueline Harper, in conversation with the author

20. www.psychologytoday.com/blog/happiness-in-world/201209/the-danger-keeping-secrets

21. www.ted.com/talks/martin_seligman_on_the_state_of_psychology.html

Conclusion

1. Joseph Campbell, *The Power of Myth*, Doubleday, 1988, quoted in *Joseph Campbell and the Power of Myth* with Bill Moyers, PBS television series, Mystic Fire video, 2001

2. C.G. Jung, 'The Philosophical Tree', 1945, in *Collected Works, Vol. XIII: Alchemical Studies*, Routledge and Kegan Paul, 1968, paragraph 335

3. Stephen A. Diamond, PhD, www.psychologytoday.com/blog/evil-deeds/201204/essential-secrets-psychotherapy-what-is-the-shadow

4. James Low, *Being Guru Rinpoche: A Commentary on Nuden Dorje's Terma Vidyadhara Guru Sadhana*, Trafford Publishing, 2006, p.72, in reference to Tantric practice rather than specifically shadow work.

5. Quoted in Joan Neehall-Davidson, *Perfecting Your Private Practice*, Trafford Publishing, 2004, p. 95

6. Lin Jenson, www.nonduality.com/hl3916.htm

7. Master Sheng-Yen, http://tricycle.org/magazine/rich-generosity-2/?utm_source=Tricycle&utm_campaign=c86263571d-Daily_Dharma_09_21_2016&utm_medium=email&utm_term=0_1641abe55e-c86263571d-307297473

8. Quoted in Daniel Ladinsky and Shirazi Hafiz, *I Heard God Laughing: Poems of Hope and Joy*, Penguin Books, reprint edition, 2006, p.44

9. Pema Chödrön, *The Places That Scare You*, Shambhala Publications, 2001, HarperElement edition, 2003, p.113

10. Robert Holden, in conversation with the author, summer 2016

RESOURCES

Here are some of my recommendations for continuing your exploration of the shadow and lucid dreaming.

Shadow Work Books

Meeting the Shadow: Hidden Power of the Dark Side of Human Nature, a selection of essays by various different authors, edited by Connie Zweig and Jeremiah Abrams, Jeremy P. Tarcher, 1990

Owning Your Own Shadow, Robert A. Johnson, HarperSan-Francisco, 1991

Shadow Dance, David Richo, Shambhala Publications, 1999

Daring Greatly, Brené Brown, PhD, Gotham Books, 2012

A Little Book on the Human Shadow, Robert Bly, HarperCollins, 1988

The Dark Side of the Light Chasers, Debbie Ford, Hodder Paperbacks, 2001

Manhood, Steve Biddulph, Finch Publishing, 1995

The Places That Scare You, Pema Chödrön, Shambhala Publications, 2001, HarperElement edition, 2003

Feeding Your Demons, Lama Tsultrim Allione, Hay House UK, 2009

Shadow Workshops and Retreats

I continue to run shadow workshops and retreats around the world and will be releasing a shadow work Online Course in 2018. See my website www.charliemorley.com for more information.

I also invite you to connect with me on Facebook (Charlie Morley-Lucid Dreaming and Shadow Work), and perhaps even share your mask in the 'shadow mask gallery' if you'd like to.

Lucid dreaming and Dream Yoga books

Lucid Dreaming: Gateway to the Inner Self, Robert Waggoner, Moment Point Press, 2009

Sleeping, Dreaming, and Dying: An Exploration of Consciousness with the Dalai Lama, edited by Francisco J. Varela PhD, Wisdom Publications, 2002

Dream Yoga: Illuminating Your Life Through Lucid Dreaming and the Tibetan Yogas of Sleep, Andrew Holecek, Sounds True, 2016

The Toltec Secret, Sergio Magaña, Hay House, 2014

Lucid Dreaming: A Beginner's Guide, Charlie Morley, Hay House UK, 2015

Dreams of Awakening: Lucid Dreaming and Mindfulness of Dream and Sleep, Charlie Morley, Hay House UK, 2013

Lucid Dreaming Workshops and Sleepover Retreats

Learning lucid dreaming from a book is like learning to dance from a book: it is possible but nothing like going to an actual dance class. Those of you who want a more visceral experience might like to check out my lucid dreaming workshops and immersive sleepover retreats, which have so far taken place in over 20 countries. Visit www.charliemorley.com for latest information.

I also have a couple of lucid dreaming online courses: a short 90-minute course and a longer 5½ hour one, both of which are available through my website.

There are also loads of free videos on my YouTube channel: CharlieMorley1.

Death and Dying Books

The Tibetan Book of Living and Dying, Sogyal Rinpoche, Rider, 1993

A Year to Live, Stephen Levine, Bell Tower, 1997

Mind Beyond Death, Dzogchen Ponlop, Snow Lion Publications, 2006

Living, Dreaming, Dying: Wisdom for Everyday Life from the Tibetan Book of the Dead, Rob Nairn, Shambhala, 2000

Conscious Dying Workshops

If you are interested in exploring the spiritual and practical preparations for death in more depth, you might like to check out the 'Lucid Living, Conscious Dying' workshops that I run with my friend Sergio Magaña. You can also check out the annual Embracing Death and Dying Day at Samye Dzong Buddhist Centre in London. See www.london.samye.org for more information.

ACKNOWLEDGEMENTS

There are so many people who deserve thanks and gratitude in regard to making this book happen.

Firstly, I'd like to thank all the contributors: Ian Baker, Rob Preece, Lama Yeshe Rinpoche, Lama Zangmo, Lama Tsultrim Allione, Justin Havens, Jacqueline Harper, Clive Holmes, Geoffrey Lantz, Angela Halley, Sergio Magaña and Steven Victor. Thanks to both Andrew Ford from Inner Pieces, and Cristoforo G for the music and music production on the guided meditations, also to Mindfulness Association UK for permission to include the Settling, Grounding, Resting with Support technique.

Huge thanks to my mum for the memories, my dad for the day we spent together, my brother for the sparring, my auntie Penny for the Isle of Wight pilgrimage, all my family and to my ancestors for making us all.

Thanks to all those who kindly read through or heard me read them various drafts or chapters and offered their corrections, advice, and/or endorsements, including David Hamilton, Rob Nairn, Albert Buhr, Fay Adams, Sandy Newbigging, Lodro Rinzler, Tim Freke, Ya'Acov Darling Khan, Ian Baker, Lama Tsultrim Allione, Ken Holmes, Gelong Thubten, Ani Lhamo and Lama Choyin Rangdrol.

Special thanks go to Rob Nairn for the interviews and introduction to the shadow, and to Robert Holden for the foreword and guidance throughout the process.

Thanks to the courageous case study crew, including Tazeem, Gareth, Maki, Maxwell, Anthony, Nikki and Keith and the mindfulness retreat veterans.

Thanks to Rob Castell for the writing retreats in Cadaques and for the constant support.

To Greg 'fybeone' Haynes for the brilliant cover design.

To Tara Rokpa Centre for supporting my three-month dive into the shadow.

To Mantis Clan, the old THROWDOWN community to whom I owe so much, and to all my friends.

Thanks to Ya'Acov Darling Khan and Tim Freke for opening the door to Hay House, and to Michelle Pilley for letting me in.

Thanks to Lizzie for the tireless editing work (so sorry for that all-nighter!) and to Jo, Julie, Amy, Tom, Tony, Sian, Polina, events Julie, Rachel, Alexandra, Leanne and the rest of the brilliant team at Hay House for all their hard work on the project. Probably the best publisher in the world to work for.

Thanks to all the people who supported the shadow workshops from the beginning: Mel from Mind Body Spirit, Gill from The College of Psychic Studies, Jane and Kevin from Hello Love, Venetia and Richard from Alternatives and Caroline from Lime Tree Studios.

To my teachers and mentors: Lama Yeshe Rinpoche, Rob Nairn, the late Akong Rinpoche, Lama Zangmo, Lama Choyin Rangdrol, Ya'Acov Darling Khan and Tim Freke for their kindness and patience with me.

To the residents of London Samye Dzong Buddhist Centre, with whom I have lived for the past seven years, and to all those who choose to take the road less travelled.

To my newly married wife Jade, for being that missing piece and for so beautifully pointing out my shadow to me even when I am too blinded by my ego to see it.

Thanks to all the people around the world I've had the pleasure of teaching shadow work and lucid dreaming to, and finally, thanks to you for reading this book. I wish you happiness and messy magnificence in both your waking and dream lives!

Although there have been many people who've contributed to and advised me on this book, I take full responsibility for any and all errors or inaccuracies within the text, and I apologize for any and all of these.

INDEX

ABOUT THE AUTHOR

Jerry Syder

Charlie Morley has been a self-taught lucid dreamer since the age of 17 and a practising Buddhist for the past 14 years, after taking refuge with the late Akong Rinpoche. In 2008, at the age of 25, Charlie started teaching lucid dreaming within the context of Tibetan Buddhism at the request of his mentor, the well-known meditation instructor Rob Nairn. Soon after he started teaching, Charlie received the traditional Tibetan Buddhist 'authorization to teach' from Lama Yeshe Rinpoche.

Since then Charlie has run lucid dreaming workshops and Mindfulness of Dream and Sleep retreats in over 20 countries, and given talks at Cambridge University and a TED talk on lucid dream shadow work. In 2015 he began running workshops specifically focusing on shadow work, which eventually fed into the creation of Dreaming through Darkness.

In his previous life Charlie completed a BA (Hons) in drama, which led him to work as an actor, a scriptwriter and even a rapper in a Buddhist hip-hop group during his 20s. Alongside this, he was the frontman and manager of a collective of breakdancers and hip-hop artists who toured extensively round Europe.

Charlie currently lives at Kagyu Samye Dzong Buddhist Centre in London with his wife, Jade. He has a 1st Dan black belt in kickboxing and enjoys dancing, cinema and surfing.

www.charliemorley.com

HAY HOUSE

Look within

Join the conversation about latest products,
events, exclusive offers and more.

 Hay House UK

 @HayHouseUK

 @hayhouseuk

 healyourlife.com

We'd love to hear from you!